Compassion with Redemptive Power

Compassion with Redemptive Power © 2020, Lois M. Tupyi

ISBN:978-0-578-73774-4

Scripture quotations are from the HOLY BIBLE,

NEW INTERNATIONAL VERSION ®

Copyright © 1973, 1978, 1984 by International Bible Society.
Scripture is presented in italics.
Used by permission of Zondervan Publishing House. All rights reserved.

Cover photography © 2020, Lois M. Tupyi

www.redemptivecompassion.org

Compassion with Redemptive Power

"The world is perishing for lack of the knowledge of God and the Church is famishing for want of His Presence. The instant cure of most of our religious ills would be to enter the Presence in spiritual experience, to become suddenly aware that we are in God and God is in us."

–A. W. Tozer

Contents

Preface

Most of us want to help others who are struggling, and I would venture to say every community has organized programs to help meet need. Yet need continues to grow and the divide between those who help and those who need help continues to widen. From my perspective, one major contributing factor is that the aid and compassion being offered lacks redemptive power – it does not lift people out of need, but rather helps sustain them in their need. Unless this changes, need will continue to grow as each generation propagates another generation of people who cannot find their way out of their need situations.

I felt compelled to write this book to stimulate internal reflection and external conversation on how we should help differently – how we are called to help from a biblical perspective. For decades now help has been more focused on relief than recovery, propagating lifestyles of need, rather than walking with someone out of their need. The philosophy of Redemptive Compassion is about the biblical call to wholistic help, helping the whole person, not just meeting an immediate need. Additional resources can be found at redemptivecompassion.org to help further educate and stimulate contemplation on how we, as God's Kingdom workers, are called to do His work here on earth.

This philosophy has not been lived out in a vacuum but has been put into action for over twenty years through our local ministry, Love INC of Treasure

Valley. Using the Love INC test kitchen, so to speak, we've been able to learn, adapt and grow as we have literally walked beside hundreds of individuals and families. All of what is shared in this book has been learned through the school of hard knocks and we're still in God's classroom having only just begun this life-changing, life-transforming call to help differently.

So many people have fought this good fight with me – too many to list. You know who you are and to each of you I am eternally grateful and thankful God brought us together on this journey of learning how to offer compassion that has redemptive power. I penned this book out of obedience to my Heavenly Father and release it back to Him to use as He desires. All glory goes to God as I am merely His conduit to bring a word from Him to a world that is in desperate need of understanding how to help differently – redemptively.

I've backed up my words with Scripture to move them from what I believe to what God's Word says. I've included many quotes that are applicable to the context being presented but it does not necessarily mean I endorse the person I'm quoting. My prayer is you will study God's Word as you work through these premises to arrive at your own conclusion. May the reading of this book further Kingdom work on earth as deemed worthy from heaven on high.

Introduction

Compassion with Redemptive Power

"Compassion that changes, challenges."

-Lois Tupyi

If we do not understand *how* God loves us, how can we expect to understand how He wants us to love others? To offer compassion that is redemptive, we must study how God has redeemed us through His love. God's holy love continually tears down the things of this world so He can build up the things of His world. This is one reason He seldom rescues us from suffering. Instead He uses suffering to heal us from a false pretense of faith, which is often fueled by a hopeless, misguided façade fed by a self-absorbed love. God wants to tear down whatever false images or idols we've built so He can lay a real foundation of love which will probably look nothing like the love foundation we've been trying to grow our faith on and serve others from.

"A new commandment I give you: Love one another. As I have loved you, so you must love one another." John 13:34. We are to love each other as Christ has loved us. His love is steadfast – it endures forever. In Psalm 136 it is repeated 26 times *His love endures forever*. I don't know what a steadfast love looks like because I don't possess it. My love is fickle, insufficient, self-focused, distracted, divided and even at times conditional. I am told to love others as God loves me which I find impossible to do on my own. I have so much to learn about a steadfast love. A love that isn't defined by feelings or behavior. A shaping love that cares not for ease or difficulty but looks only for results. God's steadfast love can as easily withhold as well as give, discipline as well as comfort, instruct as well as placate and cause displeasure as well as please. God wants us to focus less on the pain we feel when others fail to love us and focus more on our own failure to love as He loves. When Christ lives in us and we are surrendered to His power, we become capable of loving well even when the cost is great. But without Christ we cannot love sufficiently nor can we accept love completely. Only Christ can complete us.

We have strayed far from the love Christ exhibited and I don't believe most of us understand how He loved others during His time here. Our love seeks to comfort and please. It is focused on the here and now, not the future. Christ's love was transformative, holy and eternal. It was not tolerant, weak or timid. Christ was not concerned with making people feel good, but rather was focused on speaking truth in love to help people become whole. His love glorified God and did not elevate self. He was focused on fulfilling God's eternal objectives, willing to suffer and unconcerned with man's ideas of worldly success.

If we don't truly understand how God expresses His redemptive love to us, how can we successfully express redemptive compassion to others? Redemption means to repurchase or buy back. It is an act of saving or being saved, regaining or gaining possession of something in exchange for payment or by clearing a debt. In Christian theology, redemption is how Christ buys us back through His death on the cross when He paid the ransom, releasing believers from their bondage to sin and death. We are called to redeem the marginalized, but because of sin, we are all marginalized. Christ's coming to earth and subsequent death on the cross was the ultimate act of redeeming love. When redemption is offered it releases the person who committed the offense from the consequences of the offense. To offer redemptive love is to sacrifice oneself for a greater love beyond oneself, to restore someone to a relationship or position they have lost through choices, sin or difficulties. Christ came to restore our relationship with our Creator. When we seek to offer redeeming love to someone, our focus should be on restoring them to community and integrating them into, or back into, the family of God.

Compassion, on the other hand, is a form of sympathy where concern is shown for the sufferings or misfortunes of others. When you have compassion, you put yourself in someone else's shoes and empathize with them. Compassion is a positive emotion that has to do with being thoughtful and decent and literally means "to suffer together." Often it is defined as the feeling that arises when you are confronted with another's suffering and feel motivated to relieve that suffering. The Hebrew word *Za'akah*, when translated, means to cry out deeply for justice and relief from suffering – a pain-filled cry of oppression, despair and hopelessness. I have heard it said that God answers cries of *Za'akah* immediately. But I wonder if we have grown deaf to *Za'akah* cries for help that beg for injustices and oppressions to be lifted, and instead only respond with acts of compassion that meet the need but do not lift the person.

When we seek to offer redemptive compassion, we seek to act justly and relieve oppression, releasing someone from their suffering in ways that are lasting and life-changing. Compassion that is redemptive brings opportunities, through community, to regain or achieve the fullness of life God promises to all.

William Booth, the founder of the Salvation Army said, "The chief danger which confronts the coming century will be religion without the Holy Ghost, Christianity without Christ, forgiveness without repentance, salvation without regeneration, politics without God, heaven without hell." I would like to add one more to his list – compassion without redemptive power. Our culture is consumed with offering compassion that lacks redemptive power. Compassion without redemption seldom changes anything, but only eases immediate suffering, need or want. Compassionate giving, without redemptive qualities, often allows self-degrading and limiting lifestyle choices to continue – feeding into rather than relieving dependency. Compassionate love looks for avenues of expression without concern for end results. I often hear people say, "I feel for them and want to do something to help them. I'll do it out of love and let Jesus work it out if it isn't right." But God has also called us to steward our resources and to build up, not enable. When our compassionate efforts allow someone to stay in a situation and lifestyle God never intended for anyone to live in long term, is it His love? What if God's love wasn't redemptive or restorative? What if His love wasn't transformative? What if He just loved you and me, but nothing changed, would it be His *agape* love? Would we become better, wiser, more whole or complete? No – love for the sake of love will not produce any of the spiritual qualities we are to reflect as a Christ-follower and negates one of the main reasons Christ came to earth – to transform us. *Therefore, if anyone is in Christ, he is a new creation; the old has gone, the new has come!* 2 Corinthians 5:17.

Our culture is consumed with offering compassion that lacks redemptive power.

Too often, as a people who want to help, we get distracted and lose sight of the real reason we are biblically called to serve one another. We become consumed with relieving need, saving people from their struggles and do all we can to circumvent consequences because we don't want others to suffer. Our understanding of the biblical call to wholistic help has become confused with relief. Instead of our efforts reflecting what Christ taught, we have focused on the needs, struggles and insufficiencies of those we want to help. Their needs become the adversary we think we must defeat causing us to forget the greater Kingdom call. We then spend our time, resources and energy engaged in battles God hasn't even called us to fight. We think we're fighting for our rights or someone else's rights. Fighting for what is deserved or wanted is an attempt to make things fair when so much of what happens in life seems unfair. What we fail to recognize is our enemy Satan will use the things of this world to entice, distract and discourage us in his attempt to diminish our faith. This is a spiritual battle and we are fighting spiritual forces who use the things of this world to defeat and entrap us. Our enemy is not of this world and our battle isn't about what we have or need in this world. Our enemy is the evil forces, the principalities of the dark world who use the things of this world to get our attention and weaken our resolve. When we think we're fighting for things we need or deserve, we become putty in Satan's hands. We must learn to fight the right enemy using the right tools.

Scripture should reveal Christ to us and grow Christ in us.

Because this is much more a spiritual than temporal battle we need to go to the source of all truth, the Bible, so we can pick up our sword and slay the enemy. We are told the Word of God is our offensive weapon yet many of us study the Bible and still don't know our Savior. We memorize and quote Scripture yet miss experiencing the heart of Christ. We might have expansive knowledge of the Bible yet never understand the God who inspired the writings. The Pharisees made this mistake. They knew the law but did not know the One who inspired the law. *"You diligently study the Scriptures because you think that by them you possess eternal life. These are the Scriptures that testify about me, yet you refuse to come to me to have life."* John 5:39-40.

Scripture should reveal Christ to us and grow Christ in us. Too much of our current helping methods have taken a Scripture and created an action that does not get to the heart of the message. Only when Jesus was teaching did He feed people in multitudes. Though He ministered to large groups, never did He conduct mass group healings. He interacted with individuals, often eating and staying with the very ones He came to seek and to save – the lost. God's love for us is intimate and deep. His focused attention is directed at our transformation not only our ongoing sustenance. He doesn't want us to just survive, but to thrive and grow in His image. We have His promise to meet our real needs as told in Philippians 4:19, but we have no idea what constitutes a real need. *And my God will meet all your needs according to His glorious riches in Christ Jesus*. Nothing can distract God from the plan He has for our life – no need, no want, no challenge nor triumph. But what we do while on our earthly journey will impact our eternal future.

I should offer a word of caution to anyone trying to understand how to offer compassion that is redemptive and restorative. God's ways are not our ways. We don't know His mind. We don't have the eternal viewpoint. So we should not, cannot, seek to offer life-changing, redeeming compassion if we aren't first in our prayer closets, on our knees privately seeking guidance from God and His Word. Then, and only then, should we publicly engage in battle with the things of this world that are warring for our very souls and the quality of life that God desires for us. As Jerry Falwell said, "Nothing of eternal significance is ever accomplished apart from prayer."

As I prayed over how to present these thoughts that God has been pouring into me over a period of several years, I realized I wanted to tie them to a very well-known Bible story about Joseph, who certainly faced trials, unfairness and injustices. I will weave together pieces of his story as we consider ten thought-provoking premises that I have been wrestling with before God. To clarify, God is not confused, but I can be and find myself continually going back to Him for clarity and further understanding. I believe these thoughts will challenge you as they have me. I also believe if you take them to God, He will clear up any discrepancies and bring further clarity and understanding as you study.

The philosophy of Redemptive Compassion has been taught and studied since 2010 and perhaps you are one of those who have studied it. If you have not, I would encourage you to do the Redemptive Compassion 8-week study at some point. I have heard from hundreds of people who want to apply the redemptive principles as they help others, but struggle living them out. One of the comments I hear repeatedly is that while they may embrace the teaching, they find it hard to implement because it doesn't feel loving. People who are trying to respond in ways that focus and engage the person still struggle with how to respond to the crisis. It was during a season in my own life, when I was set aside due to multiple surgeries, that I felt God start to whisper in my soul that He would help me understand how He loves me, so I could help others love as He does.

I have to be honest and say that these lessons have been painful and lengthy. I wasn't a fast learner and didn't even know I was in His classroom until weeks into the intense training. I will share a few of my own personal challenges to alleviate any false ideas you might have that I've got this all figured out. I'm just a learner who feels led to share what God has been showing me because it may help us more effectively offer compassion that has redemptive power. Together, we can learn how to love one another as God has loved us.

Following are ten premises, based on the Redemptive Compassion Philosophy, which God has impressed on me to write about in a manner that will challenge us to further explore what He means when He calls us to love our neighbor. A premise is a proposition offered in support of a conclusion. One offers a premise as evidence to support the truth of the conclusion and for giving valid justification to believe the conclusion. Each premise will be stated with a "what if" statement that I will attempt to defend by building a case supporting it. It will be followed with an "if this is true" statement to challenge and help shape our responses to those we serve. Questions at the end of each section will allow you to pause and consider your own perspective on the material presented. My intention is not to give you my answers, but give insight into God's answer as you look to the Lord for affirmation, clarification or correction.

⁎ Premise ONE

"God will never – never lead you to do something that is contrary to His written Word, the Bible."

–Billy Graham

What if God wants me to accept Him at His Word without trying to reshape who He is?

But He Didn't:

I am the Executive Director of a national ministry and have the privilege of teaching and training other affiliates across the nation as well as overseeing our local affiliate. Over a period of three years, as I struggled with declining health issues, everything about our ministry and the national opportunities seemed to be blossoming before our eyes – God was blessing our efforts and it was palatable and visible. So when I started to struggle with different health issues, I expected the surgeries would be successful and healing would go quickly because I had work to do – work God had opened the doors to. When the surgeries and the healing seemed to go the exact opposite direction, I became confused and dissatisfied. There were no visual signs that would indicate God had stopped bringing us ministry opportunities, so it just made sense I should be able to keep my training engagements and gain enough physical mobility to do the work before me. But that wasn't the case at all. Some opportunities had to be passed to other qualified individuals. Most often I kept plugging away, but had difficulty traveling, getting up and down platforms to make presentations and resigned myself to sitting when I taught. My lack of mobility gave me unwanted attention and interfered with my desire to highlight God. Christians who meant well and were convinced I could be healed if my faith increased, laid hands on me and anointed me with oil. I should have been functioning like a well-oiled machine, but despite the prayers and attempts to bring God's healing touch on me, I stayed physically broken and challenged.

Most of us, when we can't understand God, want to change Him into something we can understand. Not being able to understand Him forces us to choose whether we'll trust Him in spite of our confusion or doubt Him because of it. I decided to accept, not question, what God was doing and make the best of these less than stellar circumstances. Things certainly were not being answered the way I had hoped, but unable to change them, I let go and trusted God. He had a plan and rather than me trying to reshape Him into my plan, I accepted my circumstances and let Him use them to reshape me.

There's so much in Joseph's story that isn't told, so we have to speculate. When Joseph was accused of sexual harassment it seems like His all-knowing God could have revealed Potiphar's wife's deception and cleared his name – but He didn't. When the chief cupbearer forgot all about his promise to Joseph, it seems like God could have nudged the cupbearer's memory a lot sooner than two more years of imprisonment – but He didn't. And when Joseph finally came face to face with his brothers, it would have seemed fitting for at least some of them to spend a little time in prison for what they had done – but they didn't. As we read the story, there is a lot God didn't do that would have seemed plausible and would have made sense to us, yet the story never says Joseph tried to change God's mind or the plan. We don't see Joseph trying to rework and reshape God to conform to how he would like things to go. What the story does tell us is that God blessed Joseph in whatever circumstance he was in. After Joseph interpreted Pharaoh's dreams, Pharaoh could have chosen anyone to oversee his kingdom, perhaps someone from the trusted and known men around him – but he didn't. Instead we see the curtain rise and the storyline begin to play out because what God did and didn't do set the stage for exactly what He had planned to do from the very beginning.

God's Word informs and will either comfort or convict.

Twisted Truth:

We best help people when we quit trying to reshape God by reworking, rewriting or rejecting the truth found in His Word. It seems a lot of Christians are looking for unity with each other at the cost of forfeiting biblical truths and union with God. Have we become so focused on tolerating and accepting each other that we refuse to let God define good and evil? To me, our world is turning a tepid gray where all things are starting to bleed together to the detriment of everybody. I'm afraid, in a manner of speaking, we could end up bleeding to death if something doesn't change. Even some churches seem to be trying to reshape God into someone more appeasing and acceptable to modern society.

Relativism is commonly practiced in today's world. Relativism believes that all truth is relative and everything is right some of the time and nothing is right all of the time. Relativism goes against the Bible that states there are absolute truths – truths which are unchanging despite current trends. God's Word informs and will either comfort or convict. But in our current culture, if the truth doesn't comfort the reader, rather than be convicted, they will try to find ways to twist the truth to fit their narrative, to make it relative to the times. In John 8:31-32 Jesus says, …*"If you hold to my teaching, you are really my disciples. Then you will know the truth, and the truth will set you free."* When a society rejects absolute truth, intolerance disguises itself as tolerance, when in reality there is a growing lack of tolerance for anyone with differing views.

When someone attempts to speak God's truth into a society that embraces relativism they can be seen as wrong, labeled as racist, accused of being intolerant and may find those in opposition trying to silence them. Jesus warned us in John 15: 18-20, *"If the world hates you, keep in mind that it hated me first. If you belonged to the world, it would love you as its own. As it is, you do not belong to the world, but I have chosen you out of the world. That is why the world hates you. Remember the words I spoke to you: 'No servant is greater than his master.' If they persecuted me, they will persecute you also..."* As Christ-followers, we will face persecution, but the intensity of our persecution will be influenced by the intensity of our conviction and the spiritual climate of the culture we live in. If we want to take a bold stand for Christ we can say, *Turn my heart toward Your statutes and not toward selfish gain. Turn my eyes away from worthless things; preserve my life according to Your word.* Psalm 119:36-37.

In our attempt to be inclusive of others, too often we have excluded God and His Word from shaping us. Inclusion says whatever you want to do, how you feel and what you believe will be accepted as your God-given right and we won't interfere, leave you out or try to stop you from believing and behaving as you want. Too often in our attempt to be inclusive, we have emptied the Cross of its power and the Church has been seen as nonessential in our current times. Yet the salvation message is anything but inclusive – it is very exclusive! God's love is inclusive and unconditional, but there are certain things we must choose to do, of our own free will, to receive salvation. Mark 16:16 clearly states, *"Whoever believes and is baptized will be saved, but whoever does not believe will be condemned."* God's saving grace cannot be earned, we don't deserve it and we can't buy it. Unless we accept it, seek forgiveness and ask Jesus to become our Lord and Savior, we will be excluded from eternity in heaven. Romans 2: 5-8 clearly states, *But because of your stubbornness and your unrepentant heart, you are storing up wrath against yourself for the day of God's wrath, when His righteous judgment will be revealed. God "will give to each person according to what he has done." To those who by persistence in doing good seek glory, honor and immortality, He will give eternal life. But for those who are self-seeking and who reject the truth and follow evil, there will be wrath and anger.* Do not deceive nor be deceived – God's judgment is for all and there is a heaven and a hell. We will either go to heaven because we chose Christ or live in hell because we rejected Him, and that's one of God's exclusive promises.

Absolute Truth:

Absolute truth is not created, it is revealed through God's Word and the working of the Holy Spirit within us as we search for truth, which makes knowing the Bible very important. We cannot rely on someone else's interpretation of Scripture because it could be only their opinion, not necessarily God's truth. This is not a new dilemma for mankind as misinterpretation of God's Word has been a problem from biblical days on. In 1 Timothy 1:3-7 we see Paul warn Timothy of deception, *...Command certain men not to teach false doctrines any longer nor to devote themselves to myths and endless genealogies. These promote controversies rather than God's work – which is by faith. The goal of this command is love, which comes from a pure heart and a good conscience and a sincere faith. Some have wandered away from these and turned to meaningless talk. They want to be teachers of the law, but they do not know what they are talking about or what they so confidently affirm.* I personally take this as a warning from God and whenever He gives me opportunity to teach or speak, I always challenge the audience, as I do now with you also – don't take my word on anything I say or write. Go to God's Word and ask the Holy Spirit to guide you into His truth. In John 16:13 we are told, *"But when He, the Spirit of truth, comes, He will guide you into all truth. He will not speak on His own; He will speak only what He hears, and He will tell you what is yet to come."* Once you have determined truth before God, ask Him what He wants you to do with what you've just learned. He will show you what to keep and what to discard. God alone is the ultimate authority and all of us are fallible.

Jesus spoke with authority because He could quote the ultimate authority, God the Father. Early in Jesus' ministry Satan tried to twist Scripture to trap Him as recorded in Matthew 4:5-7, *Then the devil took Him to the holy city and had Him stand on the highest point of the temple. "If you are the Son of God," he said, "throw yourself down. For it is written: "'He will command His angels concerning you, and they will lift you up in their hands, so that you will not strike your foot against a stone.'" Jesus answered him, "It is also written: 'Do not put the Lord your God to the test.'"* Satan knows God's Word as well, or even better, than most of us and will twist it to confuse and trick us. Most deception carries some particle of truth which can make it difficult to discern. It's fairly easy to detect and reject an outright lie, but when pieces of truth are mixed in with the lie, we can become confused or even complacent. In Colossians 2:8 we are warned, *See to it that no one takes you captive through hollow and deceptive philosophy, which depends on human tradition and the basic principles of this world rather than on Christ.*

God will never ask us to compromise His Word to accomplish His work

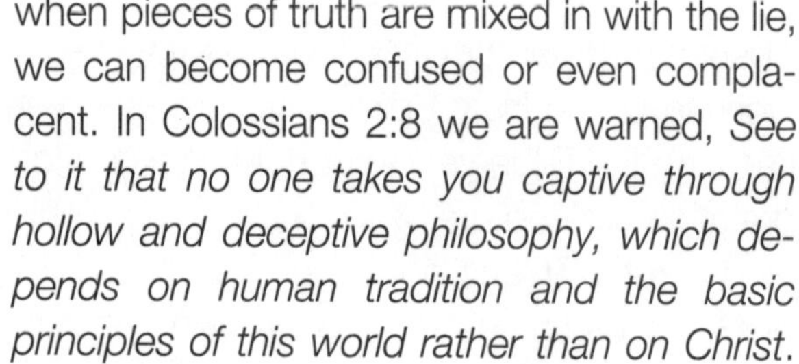

We each have a responsibility to read the Bible, study and pray over Scripture, and listen for the Holy Spirit to reveal truth. It is easy to allow someone to share their opinion of something and decide, because they've said it – it must be true. Paul warns us in Roman 16:17-18 *"I urge you, brothers, to watch out for those who cause divisions and put obstacles in your way that are contrary to the teachings you have learned. Keep away from them. For such people are not serving our Lord Christ, but their own appetites. By smooth talk and flattery they deceive the minds of naive people."* God will never ask us to compromise His Word to accomplish His work and it takes diligence and work to research the facts for ourselves. God holds us responsible to seek truth and I have found Him faithful to reveal it when I have earnestly searched for it. *This is what we speak, not in words taught us by human wisdom but in words taught by the Spirit, expressing spiritual truths in spiritual words.* 1

Corinthians 2:13. Too many Christians do not allow the Holy Spirit to speak truth into them even though Jesus has promised it in John 14:26, *"But the counselor, the Holy Spirit, whom the Father will send in my name, will teach you all things and will remind you of everything I have said to you."*

Tolerance Without Compromise:

There is so much unrest and division in our world today! People from all walks of life find themselves on opposing sides of so many issues – within families, church bodies, workplaces and communities. There is not just one right answer for the multitude of challenges facing us with good arguments from many sides. Over the years, we have seen human value distorted, relationships diminished, potential crushed, participation discouraged, dependency encouraged and spirits stifled or broken – leading to weakness, fear, depression, apathy, anger and a lack of engagement, due to the loss of hope. It appears, if events are unchecked or left uncorrected, we could be moving toward a crisis that should concern us all.

I believe the Church has the true answer of eternal hope found in Jesus Christ, but many Christians behave as if there are other viable worldly solutions. Perhaps, due to some confusion over what absolute truth is and a desire to not offend, truth is not being spoken, despite the urgent need for it to be spoken. Rather than being set apart, with clear ideals and principles that distinguish us from others, we have bought into the lie that Christ's love was accepting of sin, weak and tolerant so the responses we often give are also weak, ineffective and ignorant. We must not be deceived. In Luke 12:51 Jesus said, *"Do you think I came to bring peace on earth? No, I tell you, but division."* As I read through God's Word, I shudder at the bluntness of Jesus' words at times, especially to those using their religious position to suppress those under their authority. In Matthew 23:23 Jesus says, *"Woe to you, teachers of the law and Pharisees, you hypocrites!..."* He did not sugar coat His words when times called for Him to be strong and call sin what it is. He knew how to speak truth and love unconditionally at the same time.

We are not to conform to the ways of the world. We are not to tolerate sin, deception or the distortion of truth. Paul openly challenged Peter in Galatians 2:11-12, *When Peter came to Antioch, I opposed him to his face, be-*

cause he was clearly in the wrong. Before certain men came from James, he used to eat with the Gentiles. But when they arrived, he began to draw back and separate himself from the Gentiles because he was afraid of those who belonged to the circumcision group. Peter had drawn back, afraid of being criticized and Paul reminded him of truth. We can learn how to be tolerant of others' beliefs without compromising our own. Dr. Robert Jeffress gives us some good advice, "Tolerance means 'I respect your right to be wrong.' To be tolerant of another person does not require surrendering my convictions that certain behaviors and beliefs are wrong." 1 Peter 3:15-16 gives instruction in how to respond to others, especially those who may not be on the same page as us. *But in your hearts set apart Christ as Lord. Always be prepared to give an answer to everyone who asks you to give the reason for the hope that you have. But do this with gentleness and respect, keeping a clear conscience, so that those who speak maliciously against your good behavior in Christ may be ashamed of their slander.* We are not to be complacent or apathetic, but we also should not call people names or try to force our opinions and beliefs on those who believe differently. Methods of this sort fail miserably and do not win people to Christ. We find sound instruction in 2 Corinthians 4:1-2, *Therefore, since through God's mercy we have this ministry, we do not lose heart. Rather, we have renounced secret and shameful ways; we do not use deception, nor do we distort the word of God. On the contrary, by setting forth the truth plainly we commend ourselves to every man's conscience in the sight of God.*

Jesus loved all of mankind, but His love did not keep Him from speaking truth when truth was what was needed to direct someone back to God. He didn't get confused, complacent or pulled off mission. Luke 19:10 reminds us, *"For the Son of Man came to seek and to save what was lost"* and even in the final moments of His life Jesus said, *"Father, forgive them, for they do not know what they are doing"*.... Luke 23:34. He never compromised but always believed in and loved others, passionately pursuing those who seemed to be the most lost. As saved believers and God's Kingdom workers, we cannot look forward to eternity with a passive anticipation, shirking the responsibly to walk in His truth all the days given us on earth. To do all things with a missional mindset that is grounded in relationships and revealing God's truth as it is revealed to us, allows us to live out Matthew 6:10, *"Your Kingdom come, Your will be done on earth as it is in heaven."*

Questions to Ponder:

1. Relativism is rampant in today's society. What things can you do to help bring absolute truth to hot topics?
2. What is the difference between relativism and absolute truth? List one absolute truth you know.
3. List a few of the truths you believe God has revealed to you and evaluate if you've managed them responsibly in light of God's Word.
4. How can we be tolerant without compromising our beliefs?

Application

PREMISE ONE: What if God wants me to accept Him at His Word without trying to reshape who He is?

IF THIS IS TRUE, we must speak His truth into people without fear, compromise or judgment.

"Silence in the face of evil is itself evil: God will not hold us guiltless. Not to speak is to speak. Not to act is to act."
–Dietrich Bonhoeffer

Child of God:

Non-believers are victims of our enemy Satan - they are not our enemy. Way too often we engage in spiritual battles with the very people we should be fighting for not against. Satan takes people captive through devious words and worldly methods and holds them hostage through promises of all things worldly. They are his prisoners and we should be focused on breaking them free from his hold. Paul states in 1 Corinthians 9:19,22, *Though I am free and belong to no man, I make myself a slave to everyone, to win as many as possible...I have become all things to all men so that by all possible means I might save some.* Nothing can break the chains of Satan except Christ's love and His truth. We must recognize the enemy and understand what we are fighting for, which in this case, is to free people snared by Satan and entrapped by things of this world. We cannot coddle, nor can we afford to condemn, but we must fight with both love and spiritual truths. "Manner and message are inextricably linked; one necessarily goes with the other. Truth alone is not enough. Without grace truth is mere dogma and in the end hardens and brutalizes. And of course, love can never stand alone. Without truth it becomes mere sentimentalism." David Roper. In 2 Corinthians 10:3-4 we are told that God's weapons of love and truth are not of this world, *For though we live in the world, we do not wage war as the world does. The weapons we fight with are not the weapons of the world. On the contrary, they have divine power to demolish strongholds.* How do we break Satan's stronghold? We do it by sharing and showing Christ's love while speaking God's truth into the situation.

So many of our current helping efforts are devoid of the hope found in Jesus Christ. We assist through earthly means to meet earthly needs without including spiritual answers of truth and hope. So many people do not see themselves through God's eyes but have let their need define them. They are not what they need. They are not deficient and lacking. They might lack some things, but those things do not define who they are as a child of God. Too many people are not living in the freedom found in Christ, but have become enslaved to their need, living in adverse circumstances and bound by earthly chains. 1 Corinthians 7:23 says, *You were bought at a price; do not become slaves of men.* The best help we can offer anyone is to become a mirror reflecting who they are in Christ by speaking God's truth and hope into them until they can see it for themselves and break free of the false images they've adopted.

Part of the Solution:

A critical way to help change someone's perspective is to engage them in their life situation and allow them to be part of the solution, which restores hope and renews self-worth. Sadly, in most communities, people don't have to engage in their need situation. They can get what they want, regardless of their need, with little to almost no commitment or involvement. This perpetuates the lie that they are powerless to effect change in their own lives, as if to say they are inadequate and helpless to make a difference. When we offer help that requires no commitment and offers no avenue of participation we feed into these feelings of inadequacy, rather than helping them claim and embrace the words spoken by Christ in John 10: 10, "*...I have come that they may have life, and have it to the full.*" What current society calls free help is not free. Nothing is free and everything has a cost. Help that requires nothing on the part of the recipient ultimately costs the recipient their very freedom as they become more and more reliant and dependent on others to sustain them. This free, uninvolved help that requires nothing, does nothing to renew hope and furthers a sense of desperation. God's truth, found in His living Word, is a powerful tool at our disposal to replace the enemy's lies that they are unable to care for themselves or their families. Each person deserves to hear the words found in Psalm 139:13-14, *For you [God] created my inmost being; you knit me together in my mother's womb. I praise you because I am fearfully and wonderfully made; your works are wonderful, I know that full well*. Who is better qualified than the Church to speak God's powerful truths into people trapped in difficult situations – yet do we?

Too often, the Church is perceived as a passive, weak and judgmental group of people who push their own agendas before they care for the person. Often attempts at compassionate help may meet a real need, but can also unintentionally feed into feelings of helplessness and hopelessness because the individual in need is not invited to participate in the solution. Octana Hill says, "The church is too willing to help the poor and not willing to know them." To an outsider, it can almost appear as if the Church has a country-club mentality as an elite group of people who gather together and elevate themselves by helping others independent of involving those they serve. After working with church leaders for years I believe this perception is not an accurate portrayal of their heart. For the most part, the universal capital 'C' Church feels called to live out Jesus' words found in Matthew 22:39, *"... 'Love your neighbour as yourself.'"* Yet I have also found most attempts to meet real felt need have been clumsy and insufficient in offering a hand-up.

I believe the Church is God's answer for those struggling and we can offer compassion with redemptive power. Yet, realistically the Church has vacillated between serving well and not serving well for the last 2,000 years. For the most part, the Church has not freed and lifted-up those in need. By employing ineffective helping methods they have often propagated further dependency and suppression. I believe time is of the essence and we cannot delay. We must become educated and take purposeful, not random, steps of action, doing the work God is calling us to. A strong family unit is the very fabric this nation was built on. We can strengthen the individuals within the family nucleus by speaking God's truth and treating others as if His truth includes them. We must relentlessly seek restoration and transformation for those who struggle by restoring hope through healthy, honest relationships, built on the foundation of Jesus Christ and found through the living Word of God. Read these powerful words of God's restoring power found in Psalm 19:7-9, *The law of the Lord is perfect, reviving the soul. The statutes of the Lord are trustworthy, making wise the simple. The precepts of the Lord are right, giving joy to the heart. The commands of the Lord are radiant, giving light to the eyes. The fear of the Lord is pure, enduring forever. The ordinances of the Lord are sure and altogether righteous.* God's Word revives, makes wise, brings joy, gives light and endures forever.

Unconditional Love:

Knowing how to help someone is influenced by our personal understanding of God and His love. This was my primary motivation for writing this book. If we are a rule follower, we might focus so much on the sin that we will struggle seeing the sinner through God's eyes. This can cause us to stand in judgment of someone based on their behaviors. On the other hand, if we believe that meeting the need is the only way we show God's love, regardless of the circumstance, we can become trapped into accepting sin in order to love the sinner, which can contribute to ongoing destructive lifestyles and behaviors. So how do we balance between these two extremes? Proverbs 16:3 gives us a good place to start, *Commit to the Lord whatever you do, and your plans will succeed.* Through God's Word and by modeling Christ's actions we can learn to help well. Christ always loved the sinner but was never driven to respond to their requests because they asked. He spoke truth, without condemnation, and never placated a sinful lifestyle because He didn't want to offend. We often get confused and think that to offer unconditional love, we must not offend or correct someone, even when their life choices have entrapped them in behaviors outside God's Word. With Christ's help we can learn how to love the sinner without embracing or condoning the sin – and if we're going to love as God loves we *must* learn to do this. Let us be convicted by our faith, not conflicted by our feelings.

So much hope can be found in conviction and correction that is without condemnation!

God's love does not compromise His truth. How He loves aligns with His written Word. Christ loved the Pharisees and religious leaders of His day, but He still spoke truth and called out their hypocrisy when needed. He didn't hold back from quoting God's Word even when the truth appeared harsh and unloving. We can learn to love like Christ without compromising truth but today's focus on acceptance and tolerance has watered down and diluted truth. If we're afraid to speak truth for fear of ridicule or offense, we might allow people to stray in the name of love. Yet there is nothing loving about letting someone get off the path to God. James 5:19-20 tells us, *My brothers, if one of you should wander from the truth and someone should bring him back, remember this: Whoever turns a sinner from the error of his way will save him from death and cover over a multitude of sins.* So much hope can be found in conviction and correction that is without condemnation!

The challenge is to hold firm to our God-given convictions, yet do it with love, kindness and gentleness, treating others as we want to be treated. In Luke 6:36-37 we are told, *"Be merciful, just as your Father is merciful. Do not judge, and you will not be judged. Do not condemn, and you will not be condemned. Forgive, and you will be forgiven."* There is a difference between speaking truth into someone and standing in judgment of someone. When God gives us insight and discernment and we fail to speak this truth into someone Ezekiel 3:18 warns us, *"When I say to a wicked man, 'You will surely die,' and you do not warn him or speak out to dissuade him from his evil ways in order to save his life, that wicked man will die for his sin, and I will hold you accountable for his blood."* But when we, out of our own prideful ambition, place judgment or criticize another, God will judge us with the same judgment we placed on them. *You, then, why do you judge your brother? Or why do you look down on your brother? For we will all stand before God's judgment seat. "'As surely as I live,' says the Lord, 'Every knee will bow before me; every tongue will confess to God.'" So then, each of us will give an account of himself to God.* Romans 14:10-12. Correction without love can feel condescending and judgmental. But love without correction can placate not elevate. In Micah 6:8 we are told to do both, *He has showed you, O man, what is good. And what does the Lord require of you? To act justly and to love mercy and to walk humbly with your God.* Without the Holy Spirit interceding for us, we will fail. Condemnation pushes one away from Christ. Spiritual conviction pushes one toward Christ.

Leading Well:

Offering compassion that is redemptive and restorative requires a willingness to get involved in messy lives and speak truth when it's not popular. I think one reason people prefer resourcing the need without attempting to also build resources within the person is because it's hard and most of us are drawn to take the easy way. God despises complacency and I think, as a Christian, this is one of the greatest sin-enticements we face. We are relatively comfortable and choose to remain uninvolved and nonconfrontational in most situations that don't directly involve us. For some of us, we just don't care enough to engage in the battle. God has said He will spit us out if we're not passionate for His work. He despises the gray areas we like to put things in and ignore. I believe God wants us to seek biblical truth and stand up for it. He wants us to become truth seekers and truth speakers. We cannot turn away from injustices that don't please God just because they don't affect us personally. We can't choose to be silent because we don't want to get involved. We're either on God's battlefield, fighting for victory in Christ's name or we're not. How much must we lose before we become uncomfortable with the direction we're headed and decide we have to take a stand?

Compassion that has redemptive power takes strong leaders who are willing to walk against the flow of the crowd, without compromise, toward what they've become convinced God has called them to. This conviction requires leaders to stay determined not distracted, dedicated not deterred and dependable not defiant. Leaders must be able to attract followers but also be willing to walk away and stand alone if doing what is right requires it. If we, as leaders cannot do this, we will succumb to those around us and will no longer lead but will find ourselves being led by the cries of the masses. It takes more strength to stand up for what is right than to blend in with the crowd. In Galatians 1:10 we are asked, *Am I now trying to win the approval of men, or of God? Or am I trying to please men? If I were still trying to please men, I would not be a servant of Christ.* A leader must be more concerned about what is right than what is popular and be willing to sacrifice public applause and endure criticism for a cause they believe is God-ordained. Leadership is not a title one wears, but a lifestyle one lives. Leaders who take control by force do not create followers, they capture hostages. The true sign of a leader is someone others choose to follow when they don't have to.

He wants us to become truth seekers and truth speakers.

Offering biblical, wholistic help is not popular and it is not what the majority of people want. Many who help don't want to do the hard work of entering into a relationship with someone to help meet their deeper needs. Those who need the help don't want to be bothered by someone getting into the deeper things of their life. Compassion with redemptive power can feel both intrusive and invasive unless we have wrestled before God and become convicted to do any less is not God's best. We have this promise in Isaiah 58:9-10, …*"If you do away with the yoke of oppression, with the pointing finger and malicious talk, and if you spend yourselves in behalf of the hungry and satisfy the needs of the oppressed, then your light will rise in the darkness, and your night will become like the noonday."* Do we want our light to shine for Christ? If so, we have to put on our work boots, roll up our sleeves and get down and dirty in this business of redeeming and restoring lives in Christ's name and for God's glory. Remember, if God lifts us up, no man can bring us down. If God brings us down, no man can lift us up. We're about Kingdom work and it's time we quit trying to reshape God into who we want and let Him shape us into who He needs us to be for His eternal work.

Questions to Ponder:

1. How can we be a mirror that reflects who someone is in Christ when their needs or choices have blinded them to their potential?

2. How can active participation ignite hope?

3. It is difficult to love the sinner without condoning the sin. How might one do this well?

4. Do you agree that when a leader cannot take a stand for what they believe is right, they cease to lead and can be led astray by those with differing opinions? Explain.

⁂ Premise TWO

"We do not see the world as it is – we see the world as we are."

–James Hunter

What if God wants me to accept and celebrate Him as the Creator of all things?

Celebrating All Good Things:

Throughout this book I will share about my health struggles and specifically about how difficult six weeks of recovery were. But there was also so much I could thank God for and celebrate in this difficult season of my life. Our home had a downstairs bedroom with a bathroom and shower that were handicap accessible, something critical to my improvement. God had given us opportunity to build our home on 80 acres of land with amazing sunrises and sunsets, that I got to view daily perched in my chair. My surgery was in May, and in Idaho that means close to perfect weather – not too hot and not too cool. My home is surrounded by flowers and each day I would sit on the porch with flowers all around me and listen to the birds singing praises to their heavenly creator. All this beauty was a minute by minute, daily reminder of the God I loved and worshiped. This God who had taken the time to create such beauty and diversity in nature, was the same God who had crafted me and was now holding me in His hand. It was cause to pause and celebrate as Psalm 104: 1-4, 35 says, *Praise the Lord, O my soul. O Lord my God, You are very great; You are clothed with splendor and majesty. He wraps Himself in light as with a garment; He stretches out the heavens like a tent and lays the beams of His upper chambers on their waters. He makes the clouds His chariot and rides on the wings of the wind. He makes winds His messengers, flames of fire His servants...Praise the Lord, O my soul. Praise the Lord.*

I suspect Joseph had an attitude of gratitude or I doubt he would have excelled as he did. We get a small glimpse into his heart in Genesis 41:50-52, *Before the years of famine came, two sons were born to Joseph by Asenath daughter of Potiphera, priest of On. Joseph named his firstborn Manasseh and said, "It is because God has made me forget all my trouble and all my father's household." The second son he named Ephraim and said, "It is because God has made me fruitful in the land of my suffering."* Joseph, by now, was an important man, placed in a powerful position of prominence and authority, but he gave his sons names that would help him remember his humble beginnings and the God who was with him through both trials and fame. What an important lesson for all of us as we learn to praise God in the trials and in the blessings – for He alone is worthy of our praise!

Celebrating Our Creator:

All of us are a creation of the God of all creation. People need to know they are not a mistake and that they've been carefully crafted by the hands of their Almighty God under His watchful eye. Psalm 139:15-16 assures us, *My frame was not hidden from you when I was made in the secret place. When I was woven together in the depths of the earth, your eyes saw my unformed body. All the days ordained for me were written in your book before one of them came to be.* In the first chapter of Genesis we see God's creative powers echoed through these words, *"And God said let there be... and God saw that it was good."* God's voice is enough to bring all things into being as confirmed in Psalm 33:9, *For He spoke, and it came to be; He commanded, and it stood firm.* Let us never forget God is in control.

One only has to look at creation to see the intricacies and details of His created things. God loves color. He loves diversity. He loves variations within plant and animal species. If we don't believe it Job 12:7-10 affirms, *"But ask the animals, and they will teach you, or the birds of the air, and they will tell you; or speak to the earth, and it will teach you, or let the fish of the sea inform you. Which of all these does not know that the hand of the Lord has done this? In His hand is the life of every creature and the breath of all mankind."* Throughout His Word we see creation praising Him as found in Psalm 19:1-2. *The heavens declare the glory of God; the skies proclaim the work of His hands. Day after day they pour forth speech; night after night they display knowledge.* In Psalm 77:14 we are told, *You are the God who performs miracles; You display your power among the peoples.* In Psalm 96:1-4 we are instructed to give Him praise! *Sing to the Lord a new song; sing to the Lord, all the earth. Sing to the Lord, praise His name; proclaim His salvation day after day. Declare His glory among the nations, His marvelous deeds among all peoples. For great is the Lord and most worthy of praise; He is to be feared above all gods.* We are even told in Luke 19:40 that, ...*"If [we] keep quiet, the stones will cry out."*

How sad that we don't always seek and see His beauty in all things. How sad that we forget to give Him praise for the grand and beautiful world He created for us to live in. How sad that we do not strive to see each person with the intrinsic value God created in them. People need to hear that they are not some accident, but a preplanned miracle in the chain of life, designed for a role in the Master's plan. Nothing can separate us from His love as told in Romans 8:38-39, *For I am convinced that neither death nor life, neither angels nor demons, neither the present nor the future, nor any powers, neither height nor depth, nor anything else in all creation, will be able to separate us from the love of God that is in Christ Jesus our Lord.* Let us bring this wonderful message to all who do not know or those who feel separated from their Creator and the One who loves them so. When the world is spinning out of control, we all need to meet our God – the One who is in control!

Tribalism:

It is a fact that our vantage point shapes our perspective. Most of us suffer from tribalism. We understand our tribe, but are far enough apart from other tribes that we often don't see each other correctly. This hampers our ability to embrace and celebrate each other. Too often we let our differences polarize us as we talk about "them and us," being over critical of them and under critical of us. To dismantle polarization, we must learn to cultivate critical discernment to keep what is good and discard what is not. All of us should try to resist cultural idolatry and embrace our diverse cultural humanity, because it is in our differences we learn the most. In Acts 10:34-35 we read, *Then Peter began to speak: "I now realize how true it is that God does not show favoritism but accepts men from every nation who fear Him and do what is right."* Let us not be afraid to love those we don't understand, knowing God created them. We are all brothers and sisters in God's family.

We are naturally drawn to congregate with others who are similar to us with whom we easily relate, but to make an impact beyond our immediate sphere of influence, we must leave our comfort zone and embrace those who are different from us. Learning how to get along with and embrace, not criticize, those who are different is part of our maturing process. We must seek to understand more than to be understood and to listen and learn from each other, more than honing our rebuttal to prove a point. If we narrow our exposure to just those who look and/or think like us, we can incorrectly begin to think our perspective, how we look and behave, is right and everyone else is wrong. Perhaps that was why God confused language during the building of the tower of Babel. As we read in Genesis 11:4, *Then they said, "Come, let us build ourselves a city, with a tower that reaches to the heavens, so that we may make a name for ourselves and not be scattered over the face of the whole earth."* God heard their plans and answered in Genesis 11:7,9, *"Come, let us go down and confuse their language so they will not understand each other." That is why it was called Babel – because there the Lord confused the language of the whole world. From there the Lord scattered them over the face of the whole earth.* God stepped in to stop their self-worship by diversifying mankind, replacing their prideful aspirations with humility and discomfort. Our differences should help us grow up, rather than hold others down.

Knowing God created this diverse world should cause us to embrace and accept people from around the world, but I think this is hard for humans to do. In our uneasiness or ignorance, it is possible to judge another, not because he is unlike Jesus, but because he is unlike us. Too often we start to believe that unless people are like us, they are wrong in some way. If we believe that someone must be right, and we believe we are right, then it means the other person must be wrong. Judgment requires us to presume we know another's motives and reasons behind their actions. In Acts 17 we read that Paul did not try to overtake the corrupt government by stating they were wrong, and he was right. Instead he focused on bringing light to the darkness of the times. He did not lecture on their corruptness, but rather on Christ's completeness. Do we spend too much time fighting with our perceived enemies and not enough time proclaiming Christ as the answer? We don't need to win and probably can't win this temporal battle of evil so prevalent in our present world, but we do have work to do. We waste energy fighting battles we can't win, alienating people who are different and not enough time proclaiming and exhibiting Christ's love to all we come in contact with. As Paul states in Philippians 1:26-27, *So that through my being with you again your joy in Christ Jesus will overflow on account of me. Whatever happens, conduct yourselves in a manner worthy of the gospel of Christ....*

A Dim Light:

If we agree God is our Creator, we should want to bring His light and truth into the lives of those we interact with. In Matthew 5:14-16 it says, *"You are the light of the world. A city on a hill cannot be hidden. Neither do people light a lamp and put it under a bowl. Instead they put it on its stand, and it gives light to everyone in the house. In the same way, let your light shine before men, that they may see your good deeds and praise your Father in heaven."* We are called to bring light to dark places, to show love and witness to the hope found in Christ. Sadly, too many of us fit the description written in Isaiah 59:9-10 *So justice is far from us, and righteousness does not reach us. We look for light, but all is darkness; for brightness, but we walk in deep shadows. Like the blind we grope along the wall, feeling our way like men without eyes. At midday we stumble as if it were twilight; among the strong, we are like the dead.* Many of us do not shine brightly for Christ but more resemble a dim bulb about to burn out. Perhaps we do this unintentionally because most things look better when dimly lit. Shining God's light illuminates everything and exposes sin. Often we are drawn to stay in the shadows and out of God's direct revealing light. Truth be told, it is sometimes easier to accept a well-dressed lie, than to see and accept the stark, naked truth. In John 3:19-20 we are told, *"This is the verdict: Light has come into the world, but men loved darkness instead of light because their deeds were evil. Everyone who does evil hates the light, and will not come into the light for fear that his deeds will be exposed."* Shining brightly for Christ means we boldly proclaim and celebrate who He is and what He has done for us, without hesitation or apology, as stated in John 3:21, *"But whoever lives by the truth comes into the light, so that it may be seen plainly that what he has done has been done through God."* Rather than flickering in the dark, let us glow like a fluorescent bulb reflecting Jesus' words, ...*"I am the light of the world. Whoever follows me will never walk in darkness, but will have the light of life."* John 8:12.

It is sometimes easier to accept a well-dressed lie, than to see and accept the stark, naked truth.

I feel a need to add a side note here. Some of us like to shine a spotlight on ourselves, highlighting what we have done, rather than what Christ has done through us. This can blind the person looking on so they look away rather than looking for the path to Christ. I also know that when a spotlight is shining in our face, it blinds our ability to see others and if we're blinded and they're blinded, in actuality, the light benefits no one. Let us make sure the light we shine illuminates the path toward Christ and doesn't lead others astray or in the wrong way.

Fear of the Lord:

When we accept and celebrate God as our Creator it should, to some degree, put the fear of God into us. Jesus said to us in Luke 12:4-5, *"I tell you, my friends, do not be afraid of those who kill the body and after that can do no more. But I will show you whom you should fear: Fear Him who, after the killing of the body, has power to throw you into hell. Yes, I tell you, fear Him."* I have heard it said that those who lack the fear of the Lord may suffer from spiritual leprosy. Spiritual leprosy of the soul creates a hardened conscious no longer able to hear or heed spiritual warnings. Those suffering from this ailment can easily be enticed to turn from God's ways to the path of foolishness. At the core of this foolishness is an inability to know and fear the Lord. In Psalm 36:1-4 we are told, *An oracle is within my heart concerning the sinfulness of the wicked: There is no fear of God before his eyes. For in his own eyes he flatters himself too much to detect or hate his sin. The words of his mouth are wicked and deceitful; he has ceased to be wise and to do good. Even on his bed he plots evil; he commits himself to a sinful course and does not reject what is wrong.*

Without the fear of God, we become unable to see the error of our ways and as sin takes over, we soon become a fool doing foolish things. In Proverbs 3:7 we are told, *Do not be wise in your own eyes; fear the Lord and shun evil.* A fool is not necessarily one devoid of intelligence. As Dee Brestin said, "What makes a person a fool is not a lack of intelligence or a lack of religious activity; but a lack of fear of God." A fool is anyone who lives life without an awareness of God. Society and Christians alike seem comfortable ignoring God and twisting Scripture to fit their personal beliefs or agendas with little or no fear of His judgment. If we have no fear of God, we can fall into Satan's trap and soon become foolish people going about our business without thought of holy consequences. Proverbs 1:32-33 tells us our fate, *"For the waywardness of the simple will kill them, and the complacency of fools will destroy them; but whoever listens to me will live in safety and be at ease, without fear of harm."* Fear God but have no fear of whether your actions are pleasing or displeasing to man, for our destiny lies with God not man.

Questions to Ponder:

1. List five things that remind you of how magnificent your Creator is.

2. Do you agree that to better impact our world we need to leave our comfort zone and step out in areas and circumstances unfamiliar to us? Explain further.

3. Do you find it easier to accept a well-dressed lie than to see the naked truth? Explain.

4. I said a fool is not necessarily one devoid of intelligence, but rather one who lives life without an awareness of God. Do you agree? Explain.

Application

PREMISE TWO: What if God wants me to accept and celebrate Him as the Creator of all things?

IF THIS IS TRUE, then we must see the diversity within people as part of His plan.

"Civilizations should be measured by the degree of diversity attained and the degree of unity retained."
–W.H. Auden

Diversity:

Ethnic groups, cultural differences, race and color have always been areas where we find ourselves either identifying with or arguing about, relating to or dividing over. Too often we see our differences, rather than our similarities. I have always thought we are more alike than different. We want to have value and be valued. We want to offer love and be loved. We want to be heard and asked for our opinion. We want to be included, not excluded. We hurt, get angry, feel joy and fear. We're not so different, you and I, because we're God-created in His image. Our differences and diversity are meant to delight and excite, bringing color into our lives and our world. Our differences should complete us, not cause us to compete against each other. I can't help but wonder how far we have strayed from what our Creator had in mind when He splashed different colors, passions, skills and aptitudes into all of us.

Our differences should complete us, not cause us to compete against each other.

Even in biblical times there were divisions among the believers. Jews were the chosen people and yet, on Jesus death, the gift of salvation became available to the Gentiles also. In Acts 11:9,17 as God reveals truth to Peter, *"The voice spoke from heaven a second time, 'Do not call anything impure that God has made clean.' "So if God gave them the same gift as He gave us, who believed in the Lord Jesus Christ, who was I to think that I could oppose God?"* Who are we that we think we can oppose God and debate if all are created equal? In Galatians 3:28 we are told, *There is neither Jew nor Greek, slave nor free, male nor female, for you are all one in Christ Jesus.* And in Colossians 3:11 *Here there is no Greek or Jew, circumcised or uncircumcised, barbarian, Scythian, slave or free, but Christ is all, and is in all.* In Revelation 5:9 we are reminded that Christ died for all, *"...with your blood you purchased men for God from every tribe and language and people and nation."* When it comes to how God sees us, the value He has placed within us and the love He has for us – there is no division. We are all His children, heirs to the throne and brothers and sisters in Christ.

Mob Mentality:

Riots, revolutions and organized protests are usually a result of dislike or disagreement over something or someone and are often fed by accusations of racism, intolerance, differences of opinions and cultural oddities. Like-minded people will join together in solidarity of some cause, but the end result is usually further division and unrest. Throughout history we have seen the destruction and damage that can result from agitated groups of people trying to make their voices heard. In John chapters 18 and 19, during Jesus' trial, we read how Pilate tried to set Him free multiple times, but the frenzy of the religious leaders ignited the crowds and reason was lost. Their justification for demanding crucifixion was based on fabricated and unsubstantiated stories built out of fear. Those in power felt their own power threatened and out of fear wanted to kill the one they could not control. We see it again when Paul was under attack in Acts 21:27-28, 30, *...They stirred up the whole crowd and seized him, shouting, "Men of Israel, help us! This is the man who teaches all men everywhere against our people and our law and this place." The whole city was aroused, and the people came running from all directions....* Out-of-control mobs have had a place throughout history, and for the most part, after the dust settles, history has shown, whether wrong or right, what happened changed the course of history forever.

Peaceful demonstrations have their place and can have positive impact when well organized and conducted with respect. But any demonstration can quickly combust and escalate out of control, especially when large groups of people get caught up in the moment and respond in an emotional frenzy fed by anger or distrust. Eventually, even those with peaceful intentions can find themselves committing to and participating in acts they would not endorse or do on their own. While I'm no expert on mobs or mob-mentality, I have worked with a lot of people over the years who are dissatisfied with their own life and feel disconnected from anything important. Lacking personal self-worth they become susceptible to victimization by strong personalities with self-serving agendas. Agitators prey on vulnerable and poorly informed individuals who want to be part of something important, often looking for a diversion or escape to help ease their own pain.

Sadly, our whole society seems to be divided, whether by class, gender, politics, color, citizenship or a multitude of other class divisions and many people don't feel safe, valued or loved anymore. All of us want to be involved in things that give importance to our life, but sometimes circumstances sideline people from participating in meaningful work, developing healthy relationships or experiencing good quality of life. Unengaged people can find themselves drawn to mob-mentality movements as a place to belong, outwardly directing their dissatisfaction with life, and the anger they feel because things are out of their control. Self-appointed leaders identify and target those they can easily influence, pretending to care about them, but in reality, using them to further their own purposes. I have found people who speak with authority can be mistaken to be an authority, when they are often just bullies with self-promoting agendas. Before long, large groups of individuals become manipulated into behaviors and actions they previously would have found abhorrent and unacceptable. Controlled by fear of rejection, they remain involved despite an inner voice warning them to leave.

Individuals who organize these types of demonstrations and events often unite over division, not commonalities, and use anger and aggressive tactics to control and manipulate others. Unsuspecting, innocent people can be led astray by people who do not value them or their lives but use them to do their dirty work and wreak havoc on a segment of society. History has shown that people can be controlled if they are kept weak, under-educated and dependent on others for daily sustenance. Too much of our society has lived in chronic need situations for generations now. Our own willingness to offer assistance that does not encourage interaction and engagement, has become its own form of passive-aggressive behavior that has further discouraged and alienated people. Our current helping methods often make people feel excluded, not included, because we don't take time to see, hear or know them personally as we quickly try to fix their problems. Why would anyone be drawn to a group of people who treat others as if they are somehow a problem and broken? We can and must do better.

We can offer opportunities for people to participate in activities that promote the betterment of society, rather than revolting against society. Compassion with redemptive power can offer sustainability, rather than creating further dependency. It can strengthen, not further cripple. It should empower people to strive for their best, rather than demoralize and devalue them through exclusion. It must be willing to teach and not hinder one's ability to learn. Redemptive Compassion done well should increase one's self-worth through involvement, rather than substantiating one's lack of worth by doing everything for them. Redemptive Compassion, at its best, is uniting not segregating and inspiring not defeating. It can improve one's life by moving people out of a lifestyle of need and into a future filled with hope.

Part of the Plan:

Since all of us are created by God, we also have the promise found in Ephesians 2:10, *For we are God's workmanship, created in Christ Jesus to do good works, which God prepared in advance for us to do.* We are part of His master plan and we have a role. These days too many helping efforts act as if the helper has a role, but those less fortunate, who have fallen on difficult times, don't. Excluding people from solutions to their own life struggles implies they are too broken to participate. This lack of inclusion propagates a false narrative that their perceived failures have sent them to the bench, as if they no longer bring value to the team – which couldn't be further from the truth. Being God-created, we are each uniquely designed with a part to play that no one else can. Recognizing our uniqueness and playing to our strengths is what makes diversity such a grand thing! In 1 Corinthians 12:4-7,11 we are told, *There are different kinds of gifts, but the same Spirit. There are different kinds of service, but the same Lord. There are different kinds of working, but the same God works all of them in all men. Now to each one the manifestation of the Spirit is given for the common good. All these are the work of one and the same Spirit, and He gives them to each one, just as He determines.* One of the best ways to strengthen each other is to recognize the value within our diversity, celebrate and use it, to everyone's good and God's glory.

> We must see others, not as they are, but as God created them to be.

People sense and respond to the way we subconsciously view them. We don't have to speak our perspective of them out loud – they will sense it by our behaviors. These unspoken attitudes set boundaries of performance for the very ones we are trying to help. It is critical we ask God to give us His eyes and enhance our limited perception of others. If we want to help someone, we must see them, not as they are, but as God created them to be. People seldom perform beyond the label they are given. If we treat people as if they are needy, they will behave as if they are needy. If we treat them as part of the solution and a valuable player on the team, they will usually step up and play to the best of their ability. When a sports team is first formed, it is comprised of individuals who bring different skills and levels of play to the team. It takes time and practice for the team to move from individuals doing their own thing to a united team doing a corporate thing. In 1 Corinthians 12:12,26 we are told, *The body is a unit, though it is made up of many parts; and though all its parts are many, they form one body. If one part suffers, every part suffers with it; if one part is honored, every part rejoices with it.* There is equality of value within the diversity of function. Kingdom work is about creating a strong team of players, where everyone knows and plays their individual parts, understanding it takes the team playing together to win the game. "The most important measurement of how good a game I played was how much better I'd made my teammates play." Bill Russell.

Every person who comes into our lives is either a blessing or a lesson and both are important. Blessings help us stay the course and lessons help us grow. As we interact with people, sometimes we get to be a blessing encouraging someone to persevere and stay in the game. Other times, as we enter a relationship expecting to be a blessing, we end up receiving more blessing than we give. Healthy relationships recognize everyone has something to contribute and there is growth in learning how to give and receive. Most of us like to be the teacher and enjoy opportunities to guide and teach someone. When God gives us these opportunities, we should respond with gentleness, humility and love, promoting maturity and growth as we interact with others. It is also important to remember we too can learn from others as the relationship grows. Sam Adeyemi says it well, "The result of mentoring is not just information, it is formation. Anyone who can influence your thinking can influence your life." It is a privilege and huge responsibility to be a representative of Christ in someone's life, touching them for change and allowing them to change us in the process as stated in Romans 1:12, *That is, that you and I may be mutually encouraged by each other's faith.*

On the other hand, sometimes, God wants to use the ones we are trying to help, to shape us and they become the lesson. Often, when this happens, He uses unlikely, sometimes unkind, and unwilling people, to teach us. We like to be a blessing but often push back from learning a lesson that will cause us discomfort. When the lesson becomes more about us being shaped, than us being used to shape someone else, we can be a less willing participant. Dr. Laura says, "If you focus on the hurt, you will continue to suffer. If you focus on the lesson, you will continue to grow." We need to do both and be willing to receive both. Feeding without teaching creates dependency and relationships that meet short-term needs, but are lacking helpful instruction, stunt growth. In 1 Thessalonians 5:14 we are instructed, *And we urge you, brothers, warn those who are idle, encourage the timid, help the weak, be patient with everyone.* Kingdom work requires us to embrace diversity and to acknowledge and seek partnership, through participation, with everyone God brings across our path. He uses our uniqueness to bring completeness into others' lives – let us celebrate and thank Him for including each of us in His master plan here on earth.

Questions to Ponder:

1. How do you view diversity and do you seek opportunities to embrace it when possible?

2. Do you agree that not being involved in life can make a person susceptible to movements that make them feel important and a part of something bigger than their problems? Explain.

3. Think of someone you recently interacted with and determine if they were a blessing or a lesson and expound on this thought.

⁜ Premise THREE

"I am convinced that when a man sincerely searches for God with all his heart, God will reveal Himself in some way."

–Billy Graham

What if God is not focused on making me happy, but rather on making me holy?

The Pursuit of Happiness:

Oh, the ever-fleeting pursuit of happiness! I think I've spent most of my life chasing an illusion of happiness, only to get something I thought would make me happy and then, almost immediately, feel empty and void again. During one of my recovery times after a surgery, I felt extremely broken and set aside. Perhaps for one of the first times I had to acknowledge and accept that only God could bring me contentment and the wholeness of life I so craved. Feeling washed up and disposable, I finally faced the unavoidable fact that happiness was not even something God was focused on. That realization made me ask myself, "If God isn't focused on making me happy, what is He focused on?" His answer surprised me. I realized I could continue to attempt finding happiness in this world or change my focus because I was headed to live in His world anyway.

To clarify, I think God is delighted when we are happy, but focuses on moving us toward His holiness. God does not want us to be unhappy, but He knows for us to be truly happy, we first have to be holy. Happiness is not a word used much in the Bible and when mentioned, its definition is different from how happiness is perceived now. When the Bible mentions happiness, it is speaking of feeling a sense of contentment that is not dependent on our stuff nor is influenced by our circumstances. In the Old Testament, the Hebrew word for happiness, *'ashre*, means well-being, flourishing and possessing joy. It is most often translated to English as being blessed. *'Ashre* is used throughout the Psalms and Proverbs to describe the happy state of those who live wisely according to God's design. *Barak*, another Hebrew word for happiness also means to bless or be blessed as God gives and enables His Word to go forth, producing results such as authority, peace and rest.

It was the pursuit of happiness and the inability to find it that seemed to initially create a lot of Joseph's problems. Joseph was greatly loved and spoiled by his father. To his brothers he seemed privileged and happy. Not only was he the favored child, he also kept having dreams about his family bowing down to him, which he delighted to brag about. He was special and he let everyone know it. This created a misplaced sense of happiness for Joseph and a lot of unhappiness for his brothers.

Scripture found in Luke 12:34 says, *"For where your treasure is, there your heart will be also."* Joseph was treasuring how special he was and how even more special he would become someday. Just imagine what illusions of happiness he must have felt over his prophesied future. Oh, if he had only known how fleeting his happiness was with what lay ahead on his journey to greatness! His brothers were envious, unhappy and felt slighted, being denied the status they believed should have been theirs. When any of us begin to treasure the wrong things, we'll find ourselves trying to force events so we can take control and receive what we feel we deserve or believe will give us the happiness we so crave.

Blessings or Happiness:

I don't think many of us today link happiness with feeling blessed or having received a blessing, as the Hebrew words implied. To me, blessings often come when I'm not expecting them, like receiving an undeserved favor or gift. Happiness, on the other hand, is not just something we want, but something we quickly convince ourselves we deserve. Somehow, we have linked happiness to how we feel in the present moment. We are happy if we can get what we want immediately. This makes happiness ever changing and elusive because our lives are in a constant state of flux. When we put our trust and hope in things that can be taken from us, it produces anxiety and fear that steals our ability to feel contentment and happiness. We covet something we can't make happen, and if we somehow make it happen, we then fear losing it.

Ironically, I don't believe we can make ourselves happy or holy. They both are unattainable and fleeting in our own power. So what are we to do? Tim Keller once said, "Here is the irony: the less you're concerned about your happiness and the more you're concerned about God, the happier you get…Aim at heaven and you will get earth thrown in. Aim at earth and you get neither." True happiness will never be found in external circumstances. It is a byproduct of seeking God's holiness first and believing God's Word that what we need will follow as promised in Matthew 6:33, *"But seek first His kingdom and His righteousness, and all these things will be given to you as well."* For the most part, we have reversed this advice and focus on getting what we think will chase away our unhappiness. We convince ourselves that once we're not distracted with our needs and are happy, we'll settle down for some serious Kingdom time. This seldom happens because once we get or achieve one thing, we move on to the next thing we've perceived as essential to our happiness.

There are people who twist Scripture to imply God not only wants us to be materially successful but promises we can achieve lasting happiness! Larry Crabb gives this warning, "You must remain alert to compromised spiritual leaders who entice you more with hope of blessings than with the promise of holiness." Misguided believers can try to convince us that God's love means we will have present comfort in this life with very little discomfort or effort on our part. This is misleading and biblically incorrect. I cannot find support in God's Word that He is focused on making us happy as the world defines it. But I have found lots of scriptural references which support His intention to make us holy. God seems much more concerned with our transformation than making life nice and easy, which seldom transforms anyone. When God doesn't give us what we want, it's usually because He has something better for us. No one really knows what they truly need, only God does. Too often getting what we want, motivated by our own desires, just interferes with what we really need as told in James 4:3, *When you ask, you do not receive, because you ask with wrong motives, that you may spend what you get on your pleasures.*

> God seems much more concerned with our transformation than making life nice and easy.

Holiness:

There is no shortcut to holy living! God allows us to fall into despair so He can raise us up into His glory. Holiness is more about what we do than what we don't do. We can live a relatively good life but never understand what it means to be in the presence of God. To become holy, we must stand before God. To stay holy, we must live each day with an awareness of His presence.

The appearance of holiness does not mean that someone is holy. Most of us love the high we feel when we think we're being spiritual or when others perceive us as spiritual. Yet we can choose to neglect or ignore the painful spiritual breaking required for real spiritual growth to take place. In 2 Timothy 2:21 we are told, *If a man cleanses himself from the latter, he will be an instrument for noble purposes, made holy, useful to the Master and prepared to do any good work.* This purification work is not focused as much on the obvious sins, that most sincere Christians are trying to steer clear of, but rather the sins we could call our iniquities. Those hidden faults we cannot easily identify such as pride, rebellion, unbelief, envy, selfishness, ambition and covetousness. We must face our own depravity before we can truly seek the Lord's restorative work in our life. Allowing God to restore us will feel more breaking than healing at first. To die to self in order to be reborn in Christ is initially more about loss and pain than joys and blessings, yet purifying our self is part of becoming holy. The less we can do, the more God will do. The more aware we are of our imperfections the more God works out His perfect will in us. Our own brokenness shapes our view of Jesus. To allow God to heal us, allows us to become whole, which will then free us to see Jesus as He is, not as we are.

Holiness always precedes happiness because until we become whole through Christ, we will struggle with feeling happy in this life. If we put our trust and hope in Christ, which no one can steal from us, then things that come and go will have little impact on our feelings of contentment. We cannot lose God – we can lose all other things, but we cannot lose God. And with God what else do we need? He alone is the giver of all things. Only God can prepare and purify us so we can have the sincere love for others that flows out of holiness. 1 Peter 1:13-15,22 gives this instruction, *Therefore, prepare your minds for action; be self-controlled; set your hope fully on the grace to be given you when Jesus Christ is revealed. As obedient children, do not conform to the evil desires you had when you lived in ignorance. But just as He who called you is holy, so be holy in all you do; for it is written: "Be holy, because I am holy." Now that you purified yourselves by obeying the truth so that you have sincere love for your brothers, love one another deeply, from the heart.*

Christ came so we could experience hope for the fulfillment found in eternity, not so we could experience the fulfillment of eternity while on earth. If we liken it to a meal, our time on earth is just a sampling of *hors d'oeuvres* of what awaits in heaven where the main course and dessert will be served. Earth is just a taste, a small sampling of the amazing feast that awaits us in the next life. We should not expect to feel satisfied or fully fed this side of heaven. But I think many of us want to skip the *hors d'oeuvres* and get the full-meal deal right now. Resembling a spoiled child, we stomp our foot and beg for the Happy Meal® because we want the toy inside, convinced that toy will make us happy. But eternity and the blessings found in eternity are not all available to us right now, so we walk around feeling unsatisfied, complaining about what we don't have, rather than feasting on what is offered. We have linked our happiness to what we want and blame our unhappiness on whoever hasn't given it to us. In contrast if we possess a godly joy, it allows us to appreciate the pleasures of life without expecting them to bring complete fulfillment or satisfaction.

Questions to Ponder:

1. Reflect on a time you pursued something because you thought it would bring you happiness and later felt disappointed and let down because it either fell short or you didn't get it.

2. In your own words explain the difference between a blessing and our concept of happiness.

3. Why does the road toward holiness feel more broken than healing at first?

4. Do you believe God is not as focused on making you happy and more focused on making you holy? Explain.

Application

PREMISE THREE: What if God is not focused on making me happy, but rather on making me holy?

IF THIS IS TRUE, we need to worry less about trying to make people happy and spend more time helping them become whole.

"Poverty can enrich us because in it we learn the secret of true wealth. Being rich isn't about money, you see; it's a state of mind. There is a wealth that leaves us poverty stricken and a poverty that makes us fabulously rich."
–David Roper

The Unquenchable Fire of Happiness:

The pursuit of happiness can steal moments of joy in the present as we try to obtain something that is ambiguous. What is happiness anyway? If it is a state of mind, not a state of circumstance, condition or position, can it be found regardless of someone's abundance or lack? We cannot be happy or make someone else happy until we realize happiness is elusive and fleeting, and we quit trying to find it or hold onto it. When our attempt to help someone only involves resources of this world without including our God of the universe, we are feeding their futile search for happiness rather than sharing the answer found in Him.

Happiness often seems to separate and distract us from the One who gives us all good things, our Heavenly Father. In Psalm 107 there is a see-sawing movement between the judgment of the Lord and the deliverance of the Lord. Four different times the Israelites were subjected to difficulties due to their own falling away because they settled into enjoying God's blessings but moved away from Him. Each time this happened they would cry out in their trouble and God would save them from their distress, instructing them to *...give thanks to the Lord for His unfailing love and His wonderful deeds for men.* Psalm 107:31. This back and forth behavior of leaning into the Lord, recognizing Him as the giver of all things, only to return to sinful, pride-filled ways, causing God to induce suffering to bring them back to Him, was repeated over and over again. How quickly we forget God in the easy times, those fleeting moments of happy times. Perhaps that's why Scripture in John 16:33 says, "*...In this world you will have trouble. But take heart! I have overcome the world.*" Perhaps trouble is one of the only ways God can get our attention. Blessings can humble us and draw us close to God or blessings can cause us to elevate ourselves. Our hearts can become prideful with a sense of self-sufficiency as told in Daniel 4:37 *...Those who walk in pride [God] is able to humble.* Remembering what God has done in the past gives us courage for what He will do in the future. Winston Churchill puts it this way, "The further backward you can look, the farther forward you can see." A life free from troubles on this side of heaven will probably make one unfit for heaven.

The pursuit of earthly happiness is like an unquenchable fire that requires fuel to keep burning. The more we try to help someone find happiness through things or circumstances, the more fuel we add to the fire. Worldly happiness is fleeting and the more we feed it, the greater the appetite becomes to pursue it. Trying to appease someone's state of mind by making them happy is impossible. In Jude 22-23 we are told, *Be merciful to those who doubt; snatch others from the fire and save them; to others show mercy, mixed with fear – hating even the clothing stained by corrupted flesh.* When we become focused on making someone happy by giving them what they have asked for, we can easily lead them away from God. "Happiness is not a sign that we are right with God; happiness is a sign of satisfaction, that is all, and the majority of us can be satisfied on too low a level. Jesus Christ disturbs every kind of satisfaction that is less than delight in God." Oswald Chambers.

Matters of the Heart:

To help someone caught in the cycle of chasing happiness rather than seeking the wholeness of life God has promised, we must help them change their perspective and this will call for self-examination. The challenge is we cannot force someone to realistically examine their heart or motives unless they want to. An unwilling participant will be blinded by the things of this world and unable to detect the things of the heart. We cannot see motives. We can make personal judgments as to motives, but we cannot see them – not someone else's and sometimes we don't fully understand our own. It is our heart that shapes our motives which then drives our actions and words. Luke 6:45 states, *"The good man brings good things out of the good stored up in his heart, and the evil man brings evil things out of the evil stored up in his heart. For out of the overflow of his heart his mouth speaks."* That is why it is important to examine our own motives for helping someone, especially when our help seems to fuel their pursuit of happiness. If we are honest, sometimes our motivation is driven more by guilt than compassion. We feel guilty over what we have and so our response to their request is impacted by these guilty feelings. When guilt becomes our motivating factor, our need to make someone happy will take precedence over what is really needed. Guilt motivation is not easily identified, but I believe all matters of the heart require soul searching, which makes self-examination a spiritual matter that must involve God. *Each one should test his own actions. Then he can take pride in himself, without comparing himself to somebody else, for each one should carry his own load.* Galatians 6:4-5.

If we only address what is seen, the unseen will continue to infect a person's overall mental and emotional health. That is why it is so important that we learn how to help the whole person. Physical need and pain are evident to the naked eye and people are often quick to ask for help and usually we are quick to address it. But spiritual, emotional and mental challenges can be hidden and unseen by us initially. However, these issues are equally important in bringing health and healing to a person because the state of our soul is as important as the physical needs and condition of our body. *Is any one of you in trouble? He should pray. Is anyone happy? Let him sing songs of praise. Is any one of you sick? He should call the elders of the church to pray over him and anoint him with oil in the name of the Lord. And the prayer offered in faith will make the sick person well; the Lord will raise him up. If he has sinned, he will be forgiven. Therefore confess your sins to each other and pray for each other so that you may be healed. The prayer of a righteous man is powerful and effective.* James 5:13-16. The spiritual sickness James is referring to is not necessarily a physical ailment. Spiritual sickness includes weariness, discouragement, a hampered faith, as well as sinful behaviors or addictions. It is very difficult, if not impossible, to identify and heal a spiritual sickness in isolation. We need God and others to help us find our way back to wholeness and the fullness of life God has promised. "No man should be alone when he opposes Satan. The church was instituted for this purpose, that the hands may be joined together and one may help another." Martin Luther.

Jesus could heal the physically blind, deaf and diseased but could not heal the spiritual blindness of the religious leaders of His day because they rejected Him. Matters of the heart are much harder to correct than a physical need or healing. In the book of Matthew Chapter 23 there are seven woes listed – issues of the heart that Jesus could not touch because the people refused to acknowledge their sin and the arrogance of their religion. We can meet physical needs and never really help people who are struggling to find wholeness in life because it is not connected to the physical things in their life. Their abundance or lack of it does not define quality of life or character of person. We are not our stuff and who we are, how whole we feel, is not connected to our stuff. If we want to help the person we must address matters of the heart. I cannot think of one single *thing* that has brought me lasting happiness – temporary relief, excitement, a sense of fulfillment, maybe. But ongoing happiness? Not one thing!

Poked Full of Holes:

Before we attempt to help someone obtain wholeness in their life, we first have to work it out within ourselves. If we're unwilling or have not taken the time to work out our own holiness with the Lord, we cannot and should not try to help someone find wholeness in their own life. We cannot show His way if we don't know His way. We cannot know His way if we go our own way. The cold, hard fact is we may want to become holy, but we can't be holy without God. To move toward holiness, we must first allow God to poke holes in the self-made image we're so proud of and let Him pour out those things which prevent His holiness from living within us. Unless God transforms our sinful state, whatever holiness we exhibit is a sham. Only God is holy and only He can develop this holy trait in us. If we want to become more holy, then we must become wholly and completely His, which means full obedience and submission.

> Abundance or lack of it does not define quality of life or character of person.

How then will we help someone become whole? We must bring them into the presence of the living God, just as we must go. For it is when we stand in His light that He can shed light into the darkness invading our soul that keeps us from being whole. *For you were once darkness, but now you are light in the Lord. Live as children of light (for the fruit of the light consists in all goodness, righteousness and truth) and find out what pleases the Lord. Have nothing to do with the fruitless deeds of darkness, but rather expose them.* Ephesians 5:8-11.

The things we want or need can control us and the thing we need most can make us vulnerable to sin. Happiness is usually about pursuing selfish desires, wanting things we don't have, or envying things others do have, and it almost always steals our joy of living in the present. It often rears its ugly head as jealousy, which causes us to compare and compete, and keeps us from celebrating and affirming ourselves or others. To feel less vulnerable and out of control we should practice gratitude, focusing less on what we need and more on what we have. When our interaction with someone brings them into the presence of our living God who is the author of all blessings, we bestow a blessing on them. "To bless is to bestow something that promotes or contributes to another's happiness, well-being or prosperity." David Roper. To bring an awareness that God loves us and is present, no matter the current difficulty or challenge, is to bestow one of the greatest blessings we can on others, bringing a true form of happiness, called joy, into their life.

Ultimately, to know God and to make Him known to others, should be our heart's greatest desire. If we let this define what we do, it will naturally filter out those things that might bring worldly comfort without the presence of God. As long as we feel a need to relieve someone's pain or situation so they can *feel* happy, we'll fall short of the greater call. If we can learn to cling to the One who makes us whole, happiness will sneak into our soul and show up when we least expect it.

Building on a Firm Foundation:

Holy love tears down before it starts to build up. As I stated earlier, this feels more painful than loving at first. If we want to help someone move toward wholeness in their life, we must be willing to do things that are difficult and may not feel as loving initially. God uses whatever is needed to help us move closer to Him, but He always has our good in mind. Everything flows out of His love moving us closer into His love. To model His love, sometimes we must allow others to temporarily suffer, not out of spite or malice, but out of a deep desire to see them become whole. Too often people just want to be given what they want and left alone and attempts to help in deeper ways are rejected. We cannot expect to have our attempts at loving well, but differently, always received with open arms. We are unable to tell people what they need to hear when they are only willing to listen to what they want to hear. This is when we have to be convinced that what they want and what they need are not the same thing. We must give the needed response, which at first will not necessarily seem like a loving response and probably will not make them happy. The question we need to ask ourselves is, "Do I care enough to let temporary pain happen in someone's life if the end result means life-long gain?" To love as God loves us, we must learn to do this.

Everything flows out of His love moving us closer into His love.

If you cannot find the strength or are confused about what is the right thing to do, James 1:5 instructs us, *If any of you lacks wisdom, he should ask God, who gives generously to all without finding fault, and it will be given to him.* Through prayer, Scripture and wise counsel, God will help us evaluate, expose and eliminate those things which hinder our ability to help improve another person's life. Think of offering help like building or shoring up the foundation they are building their life on. If we just heap stuff on a foundation that is cracked or flawed, it will never last, and whatever is built on it, or added to it, cannot last either. The best we can do if we don't take the time to fix or replace a broken foundation is to patch together some additional supports to buy time, all the while knowing that what we're building on is insecure and faulty. In Luke 6:47-49 we are told, *"I will show you what he is like who comes to me and hears my words and puts them into practice. He is like a man building a house, who dug down deep and laid the foundation on rock. When a flood came, the torrent struck that house but could not shake it, because it was well built. But the one who hears my words and does not put them into practice is like a man who built a house on the ground without a foundation. The moment the torrent struck that house, it collapsed and its destruction was complete."* Temporarily meeting needs weakens those we are attempting to help because we increase their dependency on us. If the methods we use to help do not firm up their life foundation, we place additional burdens on an already weak structure.

These five rules to live by may have some merit in helping us and others move from pursuing fleeting happiness in our quest to find wholeness in life. They are:

1. Free our hearts from hatred.

2. Free our minds from worry.

3. Live simply.

4. Give more.

5. Expect less and enjoy every moment.

Happiness and wholeness really do come down to what we can free ourselves from, how simply we can live, expecting less and giving more, which will allow us to fully live life in the moment we've been given – all of which moves us into the presence of God and His holiness.

"'The Lord bless you and keep you; the Lord make His face shine upon you and be gracious to you; the Lord turn His face toward you and give you peace."' Numbers 6:24-26

Questions to Ponder:

1. How can meeting a physical need remove opportunities to address the person as a whole?

2. *Proverbs 21:2 All a man's ways seem right to him, but the Lord weighs the heart.* Do you agree that self-examination is a spiritual matter? Explain.

3. If holy love tears down before it builds up, what is God currently working on in your own life and what phase are you in, destruction or rebuilding? How can you assist someone you're helping evaluate what phase they are in?

4. In Matthew 7:24-27 we read how important it is to build on a solid foundation. How can meeting temporary needs weaken someone's prospect for a better life in the future?

⁕ Premise FOUR

"Treat a man as he is, and he will remain as he is. Treat a man as he could be, and he will become what he should be."

–Ralph Waldo Emerson

What if God isn't focused on making my life better, but rather on making me better?

Becoming Better or Bitter:

As I struggled with health issues that required surgery, I found myself also struggling with my attitude. The first couple of surgeries, both for different issues, didn't seem to relieve the difficulties I was experiencing, and I found myself engaged in almost non-stop conversations with God. I was trying to do everything the medical profession recommended and yet the results were less than satisfying. I believed God could heal me because He can do all things and truth be told, that's exactly what I was struggling with. It seemed obvious to me that God wasn't focused on making me physically well quickly. My attitude continued to plummet as I questioned God's apparent indifference and it was then I started to question my own motives. Life was good when I felt good, and I wanted that back, but somewhere in the back of my mind I felt a question start to rattle around. Why couldn't I find good in my life regardless of my circumstances or struggles? Was that what God wanted me to learn? If that was the case, to heal me might interfere and possibly circumvent the process of learning how to be better when things don't get better. It was then I realized God and I weren't on the same page. I wanted my life to get better and God wanted me to become a better person. I also knew the harder I fought, the longer the process would take. God was in charge, but He wouldn't push His agenda. He would wait for me to make up my mind. I had a choice to make; I could work at getting a better perspective of my current life or I could let my attitude continue to digress into bitterness.

I wanted my life to get better and God wanted me to become a better person.

When we read the story of Joseph, it is just a story to us. We know the Cinderella ending. But Joseph didn't. He was seventeen years old when he was sold by his brothers to the Ishmaelites and later sold to the Egyptians, to work for Potiphar. He was no longer free, but became an enslaved man unjustly accused, imprisoned and forgotten. His life went from privileged to pathetic quickly and I think Joseph had every reason to grow bitter because of what his brothers had done to him. But instead, it seemed Joseph found a way to let his circumstances make him better – something I had not done well in my recovery.

Kingdom Building:

For God, building His Kingdom on earth is more important than whatever we are building in our lives. God doesn't seem to be overly focused on our comfort or success. He seems to be focused on our personal growth into His likeness and grooming us for the plan He has for us. Most of us want satisfaction in this life more than we want to endure the equipping process God delights in. We don't want to be fitted to *live* life better. We want to *have* a better life.

Difficult times are distracting, especially if we focus on our problems rather than solutions. But good things can be equally distracting. In fact, I don't believe the abundant life God has for us will be stolen by the bad times. Bad stuff might set us back, but I don't think it will steal what God has planned. Too often what steals our joy and abundant living is settling for a life of comfort. The busier we get taking care of our blessings, the more distracted we become, and the less time we have for Kingdom things. An ancient adage says, "If you want to defeat them, distract them." The more we have, the more we need to care for and without even realizing it, we can slide into a complacent, comfortable lifestyle enjoying our blessings at the expense of growing our faith. Louie Giglio said, "Faith thrives in holy discomfort." We cannot afford to let the blessings God has given us lull us into apathy or indifference. When our gifts become more important than the God who gave them to us, we can turn our eyes and hearts away from Him and our faith will diminish or stagnate.

The better life God wants for us will never be found in the abundance of things, health, relationships or anything that takes us away from seeking an abundance of Him. God has great things planned for you and me, but most of us aren't ready for the tasks yet. Building Kingdom-workers often requires our life to get stalled so we are forced to take our eyes away from the better life we're chasing and look up to hear God whisper, "I'm going to help make you better for this life I've given you. Trust me and let go of everything you are chasing, so you can grab hold of the abundant life I have for you." Usually this will involve discomfort, loss and challenge because it seems to be one of the only ways God can get our attention – by reducing or removing those things which have our attention.

Good or Bad? Only God Knows:

Life is not a series of good and bad things. It is a series of connected events which impact each other. Some things may seem good and some things may seem bad. But we don't really know if the bad thing, such as getting stuck in a traffic jam, is actually a bad thing. Maybe getting stuck will prevent us from being in an accident. What may appear negative might be the best thing that happens to us. And when we think things are really going right, it could be the beginning of the end. If every day was a good day, we would have no awareness of good days because it takes a mixture of good and bad in life to know the difference. It can always be better. It can always get worse. Faith does not say, "I see it is good for me, so God must have sent it," but rather, "God sent it, so it must be good for me." Unless we actually believe God is in control and everything is part of a grander plan, we'll spend our lives not enjoying what each day brings, but rather rating it either good or bad and then letting it determine our mood. If you agree that we cannot know what is good or bad then it might be time to trust God and let Him order our steps and work things out according to His plan.

...one of the only ways God can get our attention – by reducing or removing those things which have our attention.

Jesus won the battle – He has defeated Satan. The battle that goes on now is a human battle between flesh and spirit. Satan has lost to Jesus but continues to try and lure us away. He does this best by trying to convince us that challenges and disappointments are because we are not good enough. As a saved believer, there's no good or bad, there's just a saved sinner in need of grace, following Christ. Good doesn't mean we're succeeding any more than bad means we failed. In John 13:7 Jesus had to remind the disciples, ...*"You do not realize now what I am doing, but later you will understand."* Jesus had just finished telling them about His impending death and then He stooped low to wash their feet. None of it seemed right or good to the disciples. It takes a lot of trust to believe God is in something that looks bad. But as our trust relationship with God grows, we can more easily accept He's in control even when events and people seem out of control. The serpent deceived Eve by suggesting that if she ate of the Tree of the Knowledge of Good and Evil it would open her eyes and she would become like God, able to know good or evil. Sometimes our need to know more than God has revealed is pushed by a subconscious desire to become all knowing like God, to exist on a higher plane with Him. When we can't clearly discern something we've prayed about that seems to be wrong, it causes us to doubt – both God and our circumstances. Mark Batterson says, "Doubt is letting your circumstances dictate what you believe. Faith is putting the promises of God between you and your circumstances." Who knows if the better life we want might be the worst thing that could happen in our development as a person? Proverbs 16:9 reminds us, *In his heart a man plans his course, but the Lord determines his steps.* God sees all and He alone knows what is good or bad so let's keep stepping in faith with Him.

I think many of us spend too much time focused on "if only" thinking. During my health struggles I found myself saying, "If only my health would improve." Joseph could have said, "If only my brothers hadn't sold me." Others may say, "If only my marriage was better." "If only I had a better paying job." "If only I felt better." The "if only" list can go on forever and can ensnare and paralyze us, causing frustration and dissatisfaction. Feeling dissatisfied with life is fueled by becoming focused on unfulfilled desires and placing blame on someone we believe should have helped us. Idolatry doesn't require a denial of God, just a decreased focus on Him. When we try to find satisfaction and happiness in something that can only give temporary enjoyment, we become overly focused on what we want, replacing faith with an almost idol-type worship of the thing we crave. Wanting what we don't have instead of praising Him for what we do have can move us out of His plan. Even if someone filled these "if only" voids, we would not find lasting fulfillment. The way to improve ourselves, regardless of the life track we find ourselves on, is to move from concentrating on our own selfish desires and learn to cultivate a liberating attitude of gratitude for what we have. Gratitude includes accepting our current situations because we believe God has allowed things to come into our lives that have the potential to improve us. When we practice gratitude we can start to say "what if" instead of "if only." "If only" is filled with regret for something past, "what if" is filled with hope for something anticipated.

"What if" statements begin in our mind and once rooted in our soul can give birth to hope. Hope fully developed will improve us even if our circumstances don't change. Just as sin gives birth to death, hope gives birth to life. If we don't like the circumstances we find ourselves in, we need to go to God for clarity. Perhaps He is doing something in us through these circumstances, but perhaps He wants us to move beyond the circumstance and ask "what if" in a new direction He wants us to go. What's most important is our willingness to follow His lead and work hard. Proverbs 19:21 says, *Many are the plans in a man's heart, but it is the Lord's purpose that prevails.*

Trying to understand God's "what if" in our life can start by saying "God, what if..." and then letting Him take the lead. There is a lot of distance from where we begin and the response, with many twists and turns along the way. Some of it will seem good and some of it will seem bad, but remember – we don't know what's ultimately good or bad. The only thing we do know when going through something is that we can learn from it if we'll submit. We cannot fully understand something that is still to come, but the closer we get to our "what if", the clearer we can see how God is using it to make us a better person for the life we have been given. "God does not overpromise or underdeliver. If we meet the conditions, He always exceeds expectations." Mark Batterson.

Destiny is Defined in the Journey:

The journey is the destination! The abundant, full life that Christ talks about is found in the journey, not in some obscure destination we're trying to reach that will say we are successful. We don't have to arrive to be fully alive and living out the plan God has for us. Destiny is defined as the hidden power believed to control what will happen in the future. Some call it fate. I don't believe destiny is some mystical ideology that we somehow magically obtain or something we've been predestined for with no personal input. I believe destiny is formed through individual decisions we make in our journey through life, and our future will be comprised of individual steps that take us where we end up. There's nothing mystical or magical about it – it's plain hard work to live out the destiny that God planned for us.

If you believe this, then you must acknowledge that everything in your journey so far has been shaping you, defining your destiny. Too often people, especially Christians, want to hide the parts of their journey they are ashamed of. Sharing our own personal pain is a prerequisite for consoling others. A.W. Tozer said, "It's doubtful that God can use any man greatly until he's been hurt deeply." We are healed to heal. The trials we grow through, our personal life experiences and what God teaches us through them, are to be shared with others traveling similar roads. Hypocrisy has no place in a true Christian's walk. To pretend we've not traveled our own dark paths and buried ghosts of past sin in our own secret closets, is wrong. The best help we offer someone must be real and relatable as we learn how to share our own imperfections without fear. No one is perfect, but God is perfecting each of us in His time and in His way.

We are all sinners saved by grace as stated in Ephesians 2:8-9, *For it is by grace you have been saved, through faith – and this not from yourselves, it is the gift of God – not by works, so that no one can boast.* None of us are worthy of the better life God desires for us. We can't earn it, but as our faith grows, the things of this world will dim in comparison to the destiny God has planned. Because of God's great love, He's put us in His plan and if we submit, we may not achieve the better life we've dreamed of here, but we will become the better person God created us to be. We can each say as in Psalm 139:15-16, *My frame was not hidden from You when I was made in the secret place. When I was woven together in the depths of the earth, Your eyes saw my unformed body. All the days ordained for me were written in Your book before one of them came to be.*

Questions to Ponder:

1. Think of a time when something seemed bad and it turned out to be a good thing. Write down what you learned through it.

2. List a "what if" statement you are hoping to see God bring to fruition. How might it make you a better person when it happens?

3. Do you struggle enjoying the journey in life because you are focused on a destination you believe defines success? Explain.

4. What is something in your past you're ashamed of and how might God use it to help others if you shared it?

Application

PREMISE FOUR: : What if God is not focused on making my life better, but rather on making me better?

IF THIS IS TRUE, we need to focus less on filling needs or fixing people and more on helping people better live the life they have.

"The ultimate goal of spiritual leadership is to take people from where they are to where God wants them to be."
–Henry Blackaby

The Fruit of Righteousness:

Rather than trying to make life better for people, perhaps we should try to help people become better at living the life they've been given. If we help someone view themselves differently, as a contributor not just needy, then even if their circumstances don't change, they will feel different – better somehow. "Partnership is the ability to work together toward a common vision. The ability to direct individual accomplishment toward organized objectives. It is the fuel that allows common people to attain uncommon results…simply put it is less 'me' and more 'we.'" Anonymous. What would happen if we quit categorizing people in two groups; those who help and those who need help? What if instead, we learn how to partner together moving our efforts from meeting needs, to working as a community toward a common goal that benefits the whole? To truly redeem the marginalized our helping efforts need to restore people back into community, not set them apart while we try to fix them or their situation. Too often, we've relegated people who need help to the sideline. We get so caught up in what we can do and give that we unintentionally ask them to step aside, as if they're not part of us. This ultimately causes division, not solidarity. Our helping efforts cannot blindly overlook the potential in individuals who also have assets and strengths. Our present-day society is overloaded with institutions and programs that attempt to fix people's problems or meet need, but ignore the individuals in need. Too often there is little to no effort spent building relationships that would benefit all. We will best help people help themselves when we don't meet their need in ways that imply they're broken, but rather include them in the solutions. To help someone live a renewed life, we must encourage them to let go of all restraints that have prohibited them from being a contributor in the past. Lack of contribution binds people to habits born out of need and developed over time. These habits can wear one down and weary the soul because they can make one feel less than whole. Bill McCartney says, "We have not come together to compete with one another – but to complete one another."

This means that righteousness must be at the core of our care for those who come to us for help. Righteousness is an attribute of God and defined as the quality of being morally right or justifiable. Leviticus 19:15 says, *"Do not pervert justice; do not show partiality to the poor or favoritism to the great, but judge your neighbor fairly."* We can justify our helping efforts because we do not say "no" to anyone, but that justification can have devastating results for those who get what they want, despite what they need, leaving them in the situation that created the need initially. Righteousness, on the other hand, is being holy, pure and upright. To be righteous means to do what is right. We cannot obtain or work out righteousness without God working in and through us. It is a godly attribute not a human characteristic. *He who pursues righteousness and love finds life, prosperity and honor.* Proverbs 21:21. To be a righteous person means we are not arrogant but possess a quiet confidence of who we are in Christ. In Isaiah 32:17 we are told, *The fruit of righteousness will be peace; the effect of righteousness will be quietness and confidence forever.* When righteousness is developed in us the fruit will be evident to all. Yet, I'm afraid too few of us exhibit a righteous quality when we help others. Too often our helping methods insinuate the helper is better than the helped and demoralize and discourage the person who appears weak. We can get so focused on making someone's life better through what we give and do, that we end up damaging how they view themselves. God can help us develop a right attitude that builds people up, replacing helping methods that build up the helper while subconsciously tearing others down. With God we can cultivate a pure desire to see people flourish as we help them feel a part of the community they live in. Let us not get caught up in the ways of the world that are futile and never really satisfy. Let us choose the better way, God's way, and enhance the lives of those we serve. Isaiah 55:2 asks a question we all should ponder, *"Why spend money on what is not bread, and your labor on what does not satisfy? Listen, listen to me, and eat what is good, and your soul will delight in the richest of fare."*

Small Deeds Have a Big Impact:

Earlier I shared how our final destiny will be shaped by small decisions made day by day that lead us to our future. If we believe this for our own destiny, then is it not also possible that how we make small offerings of help will also shape a person's future and destiny? I fear we deceive ourselves by saying;

"It's only a tank a gas." "It's only a box of food." "It's only part of their rent." "How can it hurt?" If we help in ways that meet an immediate need enabling someone to exist another day, but have not given them a chance to become better equipped for the life they live, have we really helped them overall? The reality is that most need is met through small offerings of help here or there and these small offerings add up to shape and impact the destiny of the person receiving the help – so from my perspective it matters a lot!

We live in a society that focuses on bringing resources to people rather than building resources in people. One provides temporary relief, the other provides opportunities for lasting transformation. What if our offerings of help build value into the person, beyond their immediate needs? Sowing and growing into someone takes time and is a slow process. Seed planted today does not produce a harvest tomorrow. Once sown, the seed grows through many seasons toward maturity. We live in a culture of immediacy – we want results now. When it doesn't happen, we often become discouraged and quit because slow progress often feels like no progress. We are a society of people who do not like inconvenience. Sowing and growing to improve a life can seem like an inconvenience unless we focus more on long term benefit and less on immediate results. If we strive to help in ways that will make a difference beyond the moment, we can impact not just the person, but potentially make a difference in the lives of those around them. The best way to change the next generation is to change the adults in this generation. Let us never discount the impact small deeds have when multiplied and stacked on top of each other. They have the potential to significantly shape someone's life, either in a good way or in a confining, life-defining way.

We live in a society that focuses on bringing resources to people rather than building resources in people.

Not Giving Up or Giving In:

"Motivation is communication that influences choices. Provide the right environment and the necessary friction so people can choose to change and to grow." James Hunter. What if we applied this principle to helping others? What if we measured our success, not in how much we gave or how many we helped, but how well we created an environment where people were strengthened and grew in the exchange? Accomplishing this is less about what we give and more about how we give. Meeting surface needs will never improve a life because the real needs are not only unidentified, they are not addressed, so whatever is wrong continues to fester and grow. If our help enables someone to stay in a lifestyle God never intended them to live in long-term and it diminishes their capacity to improve, then we didn't lift them up, we elevated ourselves at their expense.

If we really want to help someone live life better, we must help them improve their ability to deal with life. Violence, unrest and dissatisfaction are closely related to a person's inability to understand, process or manage the emotions they feel. When people cannot identify what is at the source of their pain, they often react in ways that are unhealthy and destructive to them and to others around them. Engaging in relationships that look beyond immediate need will allow us to begin the process of dealing with the deeper issues that drive people's reactions and emotions. But this type of help, real help, isn't usually embraced initially by the ones who need it most.

Recently on a walk, I must have been close to a killdeer's nest because the mother bird was frantically pretending it was wounded. She was trying to get me to follow her in an effort to move me away from her nest. I slow down and carefully look where I'm walking once the mother bird alerts me a nest is near. She lays her eggs in the gravel, often right at the edge of the road, and it's easy to step on the nest and smash the eggs. Walking with people through difficult situations can be similar. We can be so focused on providing relief and addressing their needs, that we don't notice the painful things in their life. But if we get too close to something they're not ready to share, they can behave erratically, frantically or inappropriately, and it's all a ploy to get us off track. Most people would rather we just address some obvious problem and leave their hidden things alone. But if we want to help someone become better at navigating their life, we're going to have to look for more than what they have willingly disclosed. It requires walking carefully, but lovingly, beside them until they realize we don't want to harm them, but really want to help them.

Many people have given up on themselves and their situation. They've learned to live in substandard circumstances because they believe they don't deserve better. They won't initially embrace or welcome our offers of help and we can't force ourselves on them. We have to wait for them to invite us in, just like God does with us. God doesn't give up on us, even when we've given up on ourselves. But He does give us freedom to wander lost, without pulling us in His direction. He lets us exercise our own free will, leaving the choice to each of us. He does not force His love on us. He does not override our choices. He waits, watches and woos us, but the decision is ours. We also need to not give up on people, but patiently wait for them to choose a better way and not force them into what we feel is best for them.

God will not usurp free will. But He also does not compromise or change the requirements to an eternal relationship with Him. This facet of God's love is one of the greatest challenges to us who want to help. We want a better life for others more than they do for themselves, which often makes us willing to compromise, promise, entice and give in – things which make everyone the loser. "To rescue people from the natural consequence of their behavior is to render them powerless" Henry Cloud. There are no winners in a game with no rules. Truth is, a better life will only be accomplished when a person becomes better at living the life they have been given, rather than expecting someone else to give them the better life they've always dreamed of.

We want a better life for others *more* than they do for themselves.

Me: Hey God.

God: Hello.....

Me: I'm falling apart. Can you put me back together?

God: I would rather not.

Me: Why?

God: Because you aren't a puzzle.

Me: What about all of the pieces of my life that are falling down onto the ground?

God: Let them stay there for a while. They fell off for a reason. Take some time and decide if you need any of those pieces back.

Me: You don't understand! I'm breaking down!

God: No – you don't understand. You are breaking through. What you are feeling is just growing pains. You are shedding the things and the people in your life that are holding you back. You aren't falling apart. You are falling into place. Relax. Take some deep breaths and allow those things you don't need anymore to fall off of you. Quit holding onto the pieces that don't fit you anymore. Let them fall off. Let them go.

Me: Once I start doing that, what will be left of me?

God: Only the very best pieces of you.

Me: I'm scared of changing.

God: I keep telling you – YOU AREN'T CHANGING!! YOU ARE BECOMING!

Me: Becoming who?

God: Becoming who I created you to be! A person of light and love and charity and hope and courage and joy and mercy and grace and compassion. I made you for more than the shallow pieces you have decided to adorn yourself with that you cling to with such greed and fear. Let those things fall off of you. I love you! Don't change! ... Become! Become! Become who I made you to be. I'm going to keep telling you this until you remember it.

Me: There goes another piece.

God: Yep. Let it be.

Me: So ... I'm not broken?

God: Of course not! But you are breaking like the dawn. It's a new day. Become!!!

–John Roedel

Questions to Ponder:

1. How can small deeds, stacked on top of one another, interfere in someone's ability to live life abundantly?

2. I said we are a society of people who do not like inconvenience. How do you think being inconvenienced can impact how we respond to need?

3. How can working together in partnership with those in need strengthen individuals and the community they live in?

4. If the standard for successful service was not based on what you gave or did, but rather on how well you worked together with the one you served, how successful have you been? Explain.

⁜ Premise FIVE

The righteous cry out, and the Lord hears them;
He delivers them from all their troubles. The Lord is close to the brokenhearted and saves those who are crushed in spirit.

–Psalm 34: 17-18

What if God doesn't want to remove me from my struggles, but waits to be invited into my struggles?

Finding God in the Struggle:

My problem was not that I didn't want or need God in this health struggle. I had spent the first five weeks of my recovery begging, pleading and searching for Him. It had become my constant prayer. My problem was I couldn't find Him – He just didn't seem to be around. After the second surgery I wasn't supposed to be up. I was to sit and rest so my body would heal. I've never been a good sitter, more like a ping-pong ball bouncing around, so this was a really big assignment. I went into this time telling myself "It will be great. I will spend this time with God. I'll read, meditate, study, pray and God and I will really connect." Problem was, I was doing all those things, but I could feel no connection with God – it was like He forgot to show up. The physical aspect of resting was hard enough, but my spirit was growing more disturbed as the days passed without sensing the presence of God. I wanted God to bring me some comfort in my struggle but as time passed, I found myself starting to struggle with God Himself. If He wasn't going to make my healing easier, couldn't He at least show up and comfort me?

As I contemplate the story of Joseph, I realize that I don't know if he too felt abandoned by God as difficult times moved him from one challenging event to another. What we do know is that his story repeats the same phrase, *"the Lord was with him"* each time something happened, as if to prove that God never abandoned him and continued to bless the work of his hands. Despite these ongoing assurances that God was with him, Joseph was still unfairly imprisoned. God was in the struggle, but He was not relieving the struggle, and over the next thirteen years God continued to groom Joseph for the call He had placed on him. His story serves as an example for us. Even when God is blessing our circumstances and we are doing our best to serve and love Him, the circumstance may not improve, and as in Joseph's story, at times may even grow worse. What God needed to grow in Joseph couldn't be accomplished outside the difficulties. God didn't change and improve Joseph's circumstances, but instead joined the struggle, using the time to change and improve Joseph for the future plans He had for him.

The Wait:

Difficulties, especially prolonged episodes, create opportunities to increase our dependency on and intimacy with God. I have found when God wants to impart new understanding or revelations, He usually moves us out of the mainstream of life. This is often done through illness, broken relationships, disrupted work or failed plans. During these times, we can experience feelings of abandonment and question our purpose or usefulness, just like I did. But the reality is God often pulls us out of the world so He can pull us in to Himself. He may hamper our ability to work or participate in the ways we are accustomed, almost forcing us to enter His presence without distractions or normal schedules. When this happens, we can waste time trying to change the exact circumstance God has set up to change us and sadly, if we get our way, we will miss His way. The sooner we realize God is doing something, the sooner He can begin working out whatever He's trying to work in us.

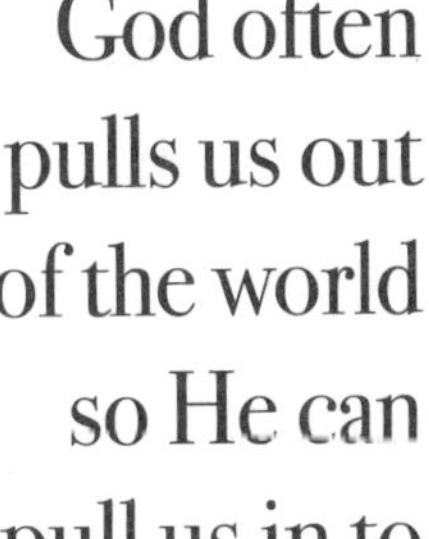

But I have also found that after we've been pulled aside, for whatever reason, He often allows us to wait for a while before we can sense His presence or He begins His work. As I shared earlier, I wanted to hear from God but didn't – not at first. What I realized later was that I was setting the parameters of how God should meet me. I had this period of time when I couldn't do much else but focus on Him, so I wanted Him to come into my schedule and comfort me, enrich me, teach me. It was all about me. None of us can command God to speak to us or demand that He brings us comfort, just because we're finally giving Him a moment of our time. Most often, I have experienced times of silence after God has pulled me aside, where He seems to leave me alone – or at least that's how it feels to me. Over time I have learned that this feeling of being alone is false. I believe He sits close by, always present, but still and quiet, waiting for my spirit to quit expecting and demanding my way. He wants me to know He is present even when I cannot feel His presence, so He waits for me to settle down so He can settle in.

David Roper said, "Waiting is the time for soul making, the time to develop the quieter virtues – submission, humility, patience, endurance, persistence." Most character development occurs in the wait. Because these virtues are hard to learn, we usually wait a long time. God is not in a hurry to start working in us, or to move us on, until we've learned the art of waiting in Him and for Him. God allows us to ask all the questions we want, but He doesn't bend to our demands for when or how He answers. Much is learned in the wait and there is much to hear in the silence. David Roper also said, "Prayer, then, whatever else it may be, is not calling God's attention to things He's not aware of, nor is it urging Him to do His duty. No, it's rather a conversation in which we speak our minds and God speaks His. We talk and we listen until we get into His mind and He gets into ours." Prayer then, is the way to get more into God so He can get more into us. Too often, once we think we have our answer, we quit listening and learning. God knows we are fickle with short attention spans, so He teaches us through silent waiting. We cannot fight His battle well until we've learned to wait well. And thus, we wait. How we wait impacts our gait. I have found God usually does not respond until we have given in, to let Him enter in.

Prayer then, is the way to get more into God so He can get more into us.

Once I realized God was in my health struggle and wanted to use it to transform me, I became confused how to pray. Should I pray to have my struggle lifted if God was using it to grow me? After much prayer and contemplation, I believe the answer is yes. Scripture tells us to pray for God to help us and to restore us. Scripture tells us He wants to delight us and give us the desires of our heart. In Psalm 116:7-9 it says, *Be at rest once more, O my soul, for the Lord has been good to you. For you, O Lord, have delivered my soul from death, my eyes from tears, my feet from stumbling, that I may walk before the Lord in the land of the living.* We should not feel guilty if we pray for relief and receive it, but neither does God want us to whine when we don't. He wants us to trust His timeline, keep the faith and continue on the best we can, never losing hope for tomorrow while we learn to praise Him for whatever season of life we find ourselves in today – including the struggles.

Listening:

Can it be that listening for God and hearing from God are two of the most important things we can learn to do well? In Psalm 81, God says several times; *"If you would but listen to me."* God wants us to listen – to come without our idols and distractions and just listen. He wants us to come without expectation and quit begging and pleading our case, because He already knows all things. James 4:8 says, *Come near to God and He will come near to you....* As a Christ-modeler, we should learn how to cultivate the art of sitting in solitude and listening with our soul, believing God is present, without demanding Him to speak in any particular way. Perhaps a common reason we seldom listen for very long is we are looking for a specific sign, an answer we can understand. When we don't get it, we get discouraged and go back to doing what we think are the important things needing our attention. God seems to have no problem being quiet when we are noisy and self-absorbed and if He needs to, He'll quiet the other voices until His voice is the only one we can hear. Zechariah 7:13 warns us, *"'When I called, they did not listen; so when they called, I would not listen'...."*

Thoughts mature in quietness. In the quiet times we can better hear the Spirit's prompting, reflect on what others have said and contemplate what God wants us to say. If we never pull away from distractions and still ourselves before God, our thoughts remain shallow because the roots are not deep. Shallow roots are watered by surface things, things of this world, rather than the rich storehouses of nourishment found in the deep things of God. Romans 11:33 tells us, *Oh, the depth of the riches of the wisdom and knowledge of God! How unsearchable His judgments, and His paths beyond tracing out!* We can't know the deep things of God unless we're willing to go deeply with God. He waits until He knows He has our full attention. If we're impatient and do before we hear, we stand a strong chance of being wrong: the wrong thing, the wrong direction, the wrong methods and probably at the wrong time. If we want to get our actions right, then we must first get our relationship with God right, and it usually starts with pulling aside, waiting and listening.

Many of us when listening to hear from the Lord have some expectation of how the answer might come. Do we understand that when He speaks all nature and mankind are at His mercy? We like to portray God as all loving, gentle and compassionate and that is one facet of His nature, but He is also powerful, mighty and loud. He doesn't just whisper sweet nothings in our ears. He will not hesitate to use whatever it takes to get our attention and get us to the place He needs us. Psalm 29:3-9 gives us dramatic imagery of God speaking, *The voice of the Lord is over the waters; the God of glory thunders, the Lord thunders over the mighty waters. The voice of the Lord is powerful; the voice of the Lord is majestic. The voice of the Lord breaks the cedars; the Lord breaks in pieces the cedars of Lebanon. He makes Lebanon skip like a calf, Sirion like a young wild ox. The voice of the Lord strikes with flashes of lightning. The voice of the Lord shakes the desert; the Lord shakes the Desert of Kadesh. The voice of the Lord twists the oaks and strips the forest bare. And in His temple all cry, "Glory!"* God can answer with a whisper or He can shout like a storm, but He always answers, even if it's in the silence.

...when we feel set aside it usually is that we've been set to *His side* for a greater working of His love

How tragic that often God must bring us to a struggle to get invited into our lives. The reality is that in these extended difficult times, when all worldly answers seem to be incomplete, we can find ourselves seeking God differently, not casually, but with an almost fanatical desperation to hear from Him. I've come to realize that when we feel set aside it usually is that we've been set to *His side* for a greater working of His love. As our desire to know Him is intensified during challenging times, we begin to better understand the phrase found in Matthew 5:6, *"Blessed are those who hunger and thirst for righteousness, for they will be filled."* God leverages the lows in life for our good and His glory. It becomes easier to fix our eyes on Jesus when the material things of this world are stripped away. Once we quit trying to get out of what God is using to get into us and give Him our full attention, then, and only then will His transforming work begin. It is after our times of greatest need we realize we have not lost, but rather gained, as our relationship with Christ grew. "Only those who struggle in confusion and wait in hope will be strengthened to struggle well and wait in confidence." Larry Crabb.

Sadly, I have found that once the difficulty releases, most of us quietly slip out of His grip, usually unintentionally, as we quickly fall back into our "real" life which leaves less time for the awareness or dependency on God we craved during the struggle. Perhaps that is partly why in the Bible we are told life is difficult. If it wasn't for times of difficulties and struggles, our need for God might become so diminished we would hardly sense His presence.

Refiner's Fire:

I've heard it said great souls have great sorrows and great truths are dearly bought. Do you agree that if we want more of God we must suffer more for God? I think our capacity to know God enlarges when we are brought into circumstances that stretch our faith. Often those who are trying to walk in obedience with God can seem to struggle more than someone who doesn't know God. A non-believer is usually oblivious to the spiritual warfare as explained in 1 Corinthians 2:14, *The man without the Spirit does not accept the things that come from the Spirit of God, for they are foolishness to him, and he cannot understand them, because they are spiritually discerned.* We can draw hope from the promise that God is walking with us and know that it is better to walk with Him in our dim understanding and struggles, then to stumble in the darkness without Him, blinded by our own prideful foolishness. In Psalm 139:11-12 it says, *If I say, "Surely the darkness will hide me and the light become night around me," even the darkness will not be dark to you; the night will shine like the day, for darkness is as light to you.* I think it's common to feel conflict and confusion as we place our faith in a God we cannot see and believe in circumstances that make no earthly sense. Yet if we only do those things we understand and can do ourselves, we may feel more temporary success, but living that way isn't much different than a non-believer and we might just hear Jesus say, ...*"You of little faith"... "why did you doubt?"* Matthew 14:31.

God sees our struggle and can do some of His greatest work when we've been broken and have become more pliable to His transforming touch as told in Isaiah 64:8, *Yet, O Lord, you are our Father. We are the clay, you are the potter; we are all the work of your hand.* It is then in His refining fire that He breaks, retools, schools and uses whatever means necessary to conform us into His image for the purpose He has planned. In Jeremiah 18:4 we read, *But the pot he was shaping from the clay was marred in his hands; so the potter formed it into another pot, shaping it as seemed best to him.* God, as the potter, is not afraid to keep shaping and reshaping us as seems best to Him and I believe correction and discipline are part of the refiner's fire. Hebrews 12:5-7 says, ...*"My son, do not make light of the Lord's discipline, and do not lose heart when He rebukes you, because the Lord disciplines those He loves, and He punishes everyone He accepts as a son." Endure hardship as discipline....* We're in good hands when we're in our Creator's hands.

When difficulties come, let us thank God that He has once again selected us for the refiner's fire. Instead of feeling neglected, unseen or unheard, we should realize we've never been closer to our Creator than when He is working out His master plan. Let us draw encouragement from Isaiah 30:20-21, *Although the Lord gives you the bread of adversity and the water of affliction, your teachers will be hidden no more; with your own eyes you will see them. Whether you turn to the right or to the left, your ears will hear a voice behind you saying, "This is the way; walk in it."* When we try to reshape God into who we want Him to be, we lose our ability to see ourselves as He has created us to be. Instead of trying to be the best "me" we can be, we mold ourselves into what others say we should be. We need to trust and "lean in," rather than pull away thinking things should be different. Our temporary pain just might result in someone else's eternal gain. Let's grow our faith as we submit and let God sanctify us in our troubles, not remove us from them, until His work is done. Then when He says, "It is enough, I am finished", He will lift us from despair and take us into His heavenly arms, comforting our soul. *Humble yourselves, therefore, under God's mighty hand, that He may lift you up in due time. Cast all your anxiety on Him because He cares for you*. 1 Peter 5:6-7.

Questions to Ponder:

1. Reflect back on a time when you felt disconnected from God. Write how you felt during it and what you learned after it passed.

2. Remember a time when you felt God pull you out to pull you in to Him and reflect back on what you learned during that season of your life.

3. Have you ever pondered that waiting time can be soul-making time and do you agree it can be a time when the quieter virtues grow most? Explain.

4. Can you think of a time when your temporary pain resulted in someone else's eternal gain? Explain.

Application

PREMISE FIVE: What if God doesn't want to remove me from my struggles, but waits to be invited into my struggles?

IF THIS IS TRUE, we need to quit trying to save people from their struggles and focus on bringing God into their struggles.

"It's not by the strength of men that battles are won.
It is by the work of God."
–Louie Giglio

Reckless Evangelism:

I think it's critically important we don't try to save people from the struggle without bringing God into the struggle, but how we choose to bring God in, is equally important. I believe there is a lot of reckless evangelism happening in our world and from my perspective, it is not taking ground for Christ. Effective witnessing about God is not based on those who talk the loudest, the longest or offer the most entertaining service or message. There are many ways to evangelize, but unless done well, some methods may serve to alienate and segregate rather than draw people in. The Bible skeptics, when caught in what feels like a one-man evangelistic crusade, may feel forced to defend a faith position they don't even fully understand and will do all they can to avoid the Bible-thumping evangelist altogether. Our zeal to deliver the message may drive our point home but miss the mark completely. Instead of bringing the hope of Christ into their struggle, we heap shame, guilt and uneasiness on a difficult situation they already find themselves struggling to get through.

Our zeal to deliver the message may drive our point home but miss the mark completely.

Perhaps the saddest consequence is that this heavy-handed evangelism doesn't portray Christ correctly and doesn't model His behavior. Instead it tarnishes His message. The life-saving message of Jesus Christ cannot be preached unless it is first demonstrated through our actions and personalized by love. The most effective way to share Christ is to focus on building a loving relationship first, and then once we've earned trust, share the message as instructed in 1 John 3:18, *Dear children, let us not love with words or tongue but with actions and in truth.* From my personal experience, if we first love well, eventually people will ask about the source of our love for them. Once they open the door, we will be welcomed to share the message of hope found only in Jesus Christ.

On the other extreme are those who don't let the light of Christ shine because they're hiding it in an attempt to not offend or make someone uncomfortable. This method is equally ineffective. To put God's saving message under a bowl rather than setting it on a stand keeps everyone in the dark. We can't bring God into the struggle if we're afraid to speak about God. And without God in the struggle to bring hope and lighten the load, it is just a very dark and difficult time in one's life. Matthew 5:14-16 tells us, *"You are the light of the world. A city on a hill cannot be hidden. Neither do people light a lamp and put it under a bowl. Instead they put it on its stand, and it gives light to everyone in the house. In the same way, let your light shine before men, that they may see your good deeds and praise your Father in heaven."* As a Christian we are told, *We are therefore Christ's ambassadors, as though God were making His appeal through us*.... 2 Corinthians 5:20. The word ambassador means an accredited diplomat, sent by a country as its official representative. As someone who helps others, if we try to solve their struggle, rather than bring God into their struggle, we become a poor advocate for God.

One of the best ways to bring God into someone's struggle is to share a personal story of a time in our own life when God came into a struggle we were experiencing. Testimonies usually come from a time of testing and are a first-hand story of how we have experienced God's faithfulness. Once we've passed the test, so to speak, this personal story, when shared, brings opportunities to offer encouragement and hope to others. I believe it is human nature to think, "If God did that for them, perhaps there is hope in my situation also." As Jonathan said in 1 Samuel 14:6 during a time of struggle, *"...Perhaps the Lord will act in our behalf. Nothing can hinder the Lord from saving, whether by many or by few."* His words were drawn from past experiences of God's faithfulness and as he shared, he not only renewed his own strength, but gave strength and hope to his young armor-bearer. Testimonies have the potential to open hearts to Christ and when we share our faith publicly it touches the hearts of those who watch privately.

Putting Christ on Exhibit:

When someone asks us for help, do we try to be seen as someone with great wisdom or do we point them to God, the source of true wisdom? I think it serves our egos to be sought after as someone who hears from God and has His answers. While God can use us in giving the answer, whatever we say or do will fall short if those we help are not also drawn into the presence of our living God. This is not easily done. Rather than us attempting to be the one with all the answers, how do we encourage others to seek answers from God? One way is to slow down our responses and change our priorities. If we're focused on relieving the struggle, then we're focused on the problem and all advice will steer toward worldly solutions to their earthly struggle. But if we believe the most important thing we can do for someone is to bring Christ into their struggle, our focus shifts to the person, believing God has crossed our paths so He can touch them through us. One solution positions us to be seen as the one of saves them and the other method brings one into the presence of the true living Savior. John Piper says, "I cannot show them the way, but I can show them God." We should not strive to be the answer as much as we strive to show them our God. We will do this best with less words and more loving actions.

We should not strive to be the answer as much as we strive to show them our God.

It's so easy to tell people what they need to do without allowing them to be part of the conversation. Speaking what we call truth doesn't make it a spiritual truth until it is filtered through God by the listener. Everyone has a part to play – those who speak and those who listen. Without God in the mix it is just flawed humans speaking and listening to each other's opinions. In today's culture, too much is accepted without contemplation or challenge. Only God can reveal truth and remove the dross. We are told in Proverbs 18:17, *The first to present his case seems right, till another comes forward and questions him.* Most problems can only be solved in the presence of God because they need revelation as well as education. Too often we try to reason with our head when we need to engage our heart also. I am not talking about reckless, emotional behavior. James 1:19 instructs ...*Everyone should be quick to listen, slow to speak and slow to become angry.* If we emotionally attack things without engaging the Holy Spirit, we may give a passionate response, but leave God completely out of the picture. There are plenty of people around who react without engaging God. As God's children, let us behave differently and think before we speak. We are told to say less not more and in Proverbs 17:27 we read, *A man of knowledge uses words with restraint, and a man of understanding is even-tempered.* We need to capture our words, setting them before God for purification, before spewing them out to others as 2 Corinthians 10:4-5 suggests, ...*We demolish arguments and every pretension that sets itself up against the knowledge of God, and we take captive every thought to make it obedient to Christ.* It's much easier to fix a problem or fill a need than to live out our faith using few words and responding only when God prompts us. Matthew 12:36-37 warns us about careless words, *"But I tell you that men will have to give account on the day of judgment for every careless word they have spoken. For by your words you will be acquitted, and by your words you will be condemned."*

Into the Struggle:

Most of us are problem solvers rather than people changers. Too often when things go wrong and we find ourselves or someone else in a struggle, we focus on the problem, rather than the person. When we focus on immediate relief it can compromise or circumvent opportunities for lasting change and interfere in God's transforming work. Rather than looking for life-changing opportunities by asking, "God, what do you want me to do in this?" we work to change the situation or fix the problem. If we want to model the deep *agape* love God shows us, we need to be able to bring God into the struggle without expecting the struggle to go away.

Bringing God into the struggle is not done easily. When life is good and uncomplicated, it's hard to convince someone they need Christ. When life is unfair or difficult, it's hard to convince someone Christ cares. For most of us, our mind and heart will only come to Christ when it appears as if all other doors have closed. How do we walk with someone, but not interfere as the doors close, one by one, narrowing their options of escape? I think it's important we understand that God's love always wants what is best for our personal growth and if that involves pain and suffering, He not only allows it, but will use it to shape us. I don't think God removes temporary suffering that is necessary for achieving His long-term plan. His love is so deep that He'll use all things and any means necessary to eradicate sin in our lives. He is not afraid to allow hurt, devastation or loss to come into our lives if the end product will remove sin and draw us closer to Him.

Sometimes, through wisdom found in prayer and consultation with others, we will discern that the circumstances of someone's choices must play out because it is a part of God's cleansing, growing process. Then we must be able to allow temporary pain for long-term gain as we walk with them in the struggle, not necessarily out of the struggle, working hard to not interfere in what God is doing. To do this walking beside someone, without fixing the problem means we should expect and be ready to accept the pain which may be inflicted on us by those we attempt to help – all because we choose to model Christ's love. It's human nature when in pain, to inflict pain, especially when we can't get what we think will relieve the pain. For those of us who want to offer compassion with redemptive power, we must realize we are not in a popularity contest. We're about Kingdom work and Kingdom work is never accomplished without great opposition, even from those we help.

Questions to Ponder:

1. What method have you found most effective when sharing Christ with someone?

2. When you have helped in the past, what was your main focus, solving the problem and relieving the struggle or bringing God into the struggle?

3. Would you say you've been a problem solver more than a people changer in the past? What would it take for you to offer help differently?

4. How is it possible to walk with someone in their struggle without attempting to relieve the struggle, unless led by God? Explain.

⁕ Premise SIX

"There is no gospel without the cross, no obedience without servanthood, no spiritual formation without suffering."

–Larry Crabb

What if most of my difficult challenges are not Satan trying to harm me, but God trying to shape me?

The Plan:

From my earliest memories, even as a pre-teen, I had an awareness that God had a call on my life – something He would do through me in an important work for Him. The call intensified in the late 1990's and when I finally stepped into the ministry of Love INC I felt I had found my life calling. I was naïve in Kingdom work to say the least and little did I know that being about the plan didn't mean things would fall into place or go smoothly. Through the years the ministry has faced closures, financial and leadership difficulties, lawsuits and disappointments among a long list of challenges that have tested our faith – but we have persevered. When my health challenges mounted, with some unexpected setbacks, I found myself once again questioning if I would be able to do what I thought God had called me to. Could God be changing His plans for me midstream? There was so much I had felt led by God to start and I had faithfully, with great expectation, been waiting for Him to bring these promises to fruition. Could He be pulling me out now, before His promises came to life? I found myself studying the faith scriptures found in Hebrews, especially 11:39 *These were all commended for their faith, yet none of them received what had been promised.* I started to wonder if I was going to join the ranks of other believers who did not live to see their promises from God fulfilled.

Joseph too had been given dreams and visions of the position he would have at some time in his future. But the road to stardom – who would have thought! Let's pretend for a moment that everything that happened to Joseph was part of God's plan. It seems improbable doesn't it? Attempted murder, slavery, attempted sexual entrapment, promises made but forgotten are a few – it's quite the list to say the least. We don't know how much of Joseph's early years God coordinated or how many of the events God turned around for good because Joseph loved Him. But it does all seem to have been worked into the plan God had for Joseph. I can't help but wonder how Joseph stayed encouraged as one wrongful event after another happened. Thirteen years was a long time to continue to believe God had a plan, a big plan, when the only one who appeared to be bowing down was Joseph himself.

Spiritual Warfare:

In the past when I have faced major struggles or things seemed to be falling apart, I would often say I was under a spiritual attack by Satan. And I might have been right, after all spiritual warfare is real and scriptural. In Ephesians 6:12 we are told, *For our struggle is not against flesh and blood, but against the rulers, against the authorities, against the powers of this dark world and against the spiritual forces of evil in the heavenly realms.* We face spiritual battles on a daily basis and we must never let our guard down as 1 Peter 5:8 warns us, *…Your enemy the devil prowls around like a roaring lion looking for someone to devour.* As I've matured and also, as God has shown me through my trying times, my immediate need to place blame on Satan, in reality has helped me shift responsibility off myself and onto something(one) I couldn't control. This blaming game has done little to strengthen me but has fed my ego by claiming that what has gone wrong is not my fault. When we can blame someone else for something we're struggling through, we feel better because it takes the responsibility off our shoulders. But that can also stunt our own spiritual growth.

I think many of us tend to view difficulties, struggles and suffering as Satan's attacks rather than God's refining work. But Scripture in 1 Peter 1:6-7 tells us differently, *In this you greatly rejoice, though now for a little while you may have had to suffer grief in all kinds of trials. These have come so that your faith – of greater worth than gold, which perishes even though refined by fire – may be proved genuine and may result in praise, glory and honor when Jesus Christ is revealed.* Perhaps suffering is more a matter of perspective and perspective shapes our reality. Is it suffering or is it learning? Do I want Christ without the cost of the cross? Do I want the gain without the pain? If we want to become Christ-like we will suffer as Christ did as told to us in Philippians 1:29, *For it has been granted to you on behalf of Christ not only to believe on Him, but also to suffer for Him.* In hard times, we will either learn as we push through, or resist the process and settle for less than Christ has planned for us. What would happen if we changed our perspective from feeling attacked to believing we have been selected by God for some refining work? Would we carry our struggles differently if we thought they were in God's hand and part of His plan? C.H. Spurgeon offers these words of encouragement, "Fear not, Christian; Jesus is with thee. In all thy fiery trials, His presence is both thy comfort and safety. He will never leave one whom He has chosen for His own. 'Fear not, for I am with thee,' is His sure word of promise to His chosen ones in 'the furnace of affliction.'"

Now don't put this book down to go tell your friend that I just said spiritual attacks aren't a big deal. The truth is quite the contrary. Spiritual attacks occur regularly and they can defeat us, depending on how we respond. What I'm trying to say is that in spite of spiritual warfare, we have to behave and act in a responsible way, not passing blame but claiming victory in Christ's name. Satan can't win anything unless we let Him. God still sits on the throne! It's good to remind ourselves that even if it is Satan trying to harm us, God can use it to strengthen us if we'll just look to Him and draw strength from Him. Crying to others about how horrific the spiritual attacks have been, might bring some relief or comfort, but the grander plan is found in Ephesians 6:13 where we are instructed to cry out to God and, *...stand your ground, and after you have done everything, to stand.* The more things seem hopelessly evil and out of control, the more hopeful we must remain because nothing can thwart God's plan. A pastor friend often reminds me that the only thing God cannot do is fail.

Suffering with Christ:

Can any of us grow into Christ's image without some sort of suffering, hardship or difficulty? My personal belief is that in our life journey we will experience challenges a few times, if not a lot of the time. Just as Christ had to suffer to advance God's Kingdom, we also will have to endure suffering to advance Christ's Kingdom. In Romans 8:16-18 we read, *The Spirit Himself testifies with our spirit that we are God's children. Now if we are children, then we are heirs – heirs of God and co-heirs with Christ, if indeed we share in His sufferings in order that we may also share in His glory. I consider that our present sufferings are not worth comparing with the glory that will be revealed in us.* I think suffering is part of the eternal plan. Our suffering is not out of God's hand but has passed through His hand to be used in His plan. God calls us to continue the work Christ began and in 2 Corinthians 4:7-9 we are told, *But we have this treasure in jars of clay to show that this all-surpassing power is from God and not from us. We are hard pressed on every side, but not crushed; perplexed, but not in despair; persecuted, but not abandoned; struck down, but not destroyed*. Struggles and suffering correctly carried should glorify God, not just after the fact, but during the storm.

Some of us falsely believe our suffering would stop if we could just live our life better, but most suffering is not punishment for a sin we've committed. Sometimes our struggles are the consequence of choices we've made, but often they are not. In John 9:1-3 we read this story, *As He went along, He saw a man blind from birth. His disciples asked Him, "Rabbi, who sinned, this man or his parents, that he was born blind?" "Neither this man nor his parents sinned," said Jesus, "but this happened so that the work of God might be displayed in his life."* The disciples wanted to attach the struggle to sin, but Jesus clarified it would be used to bring God glory. God uses suffering to refine us, not to punish us, regardless of how it may seem. We are told in Romans 3:23-24. *For all have sinned and fall short of the glory of God, and are justified freely by His grace through the redemption that came by Christ Jesus.* We are all sinners in need of grace and whether suffering is a result of our behavior or an undeserved hardship, it is universal and if submitted to God, will be used for our good and His glory. In John 16:33 we are told, *"...In this world you will have trouble. But take heart! I have overcome the world."*

Our suffering is not out of God's hand but has passed through His hand to be used in His plan.

God and Satan use opposite methods to accomplish their work. Satan tries to entice us through the things of this world, feeding into our insatiable appetite for more, by bombarding us with false promises of wealth, power and fame. God, on the other hand, wants to move us beyond the things of this world, so He often allows things to be removed, one by one, until it seems He is all we have left. For those who reject God and are madly chasing what Satan has dangled in front of them, God waits. He allows these lost, confused souls to exercise their own free will. On the surface it may seem as if they're having more success and their life seems less full of trials, but Larry Crabb says, "Presuming that everything that looks okay on the surface is okay, blinds you to your real problems." The judgment day will come for each of us and it's better to be in God's refining fire today, than to be left alone in the scrap heap of false promises and glittery things that lead us toward the path of eternal damnation and destruction in our future. In Matthew 6:19-21 we are told *"Do not store up for yourselves treasures on earth, where moth and rust destroy, and where thieves break in and steal. But store up for yourselves treasures in heaven, where moth and rust do not destroy, and where thieves do not break in and steal. For where your treasure is, there your heart will be also."*

Fence Sitting:

God has built us to succeed in life but when we try to love God and live life according to worldly standards, it can seem like we've been programmed to fail because worldly success and eternal perspectives are at odds with each other. We can't have both. In Matthew 6:24 we are told, *"No one can serve two masters. Either he will hate the one and love the other, or he will be devoted to the one and despise the other. You cannot serve both God and Money."* There is no fence sitting in Kingdom matters. God warns us in Revelation 3:15-17 *"I know your deeds, that you are neither cold nor hot. I wish you were either one or the other! So, because you are lukewarm – neither hot nor cold – I am about to spit you out of my mouth. You say, 'I am rich; I have acquired wealth and do not need a thing.' But you do not realize that you are wretched, pitiful, poor, blind and naked."* When we take our eyes off God's plan and try to live up to man's perceptions, accusations or expectations, we stand to lose everything. If God spits us out, Satan stands by to suck us in, trying to keep us trapped by feeding into an ever-increasing appetite for the things of this world that cannot be appeased. The harder we try the more we can feel like a failure. There is no compromised, middle ground for a Christ-follower. We are not who others say we are, we are who God says we are. God's ultimate plan is to transform us into the image of Christ, to work out His holiness in us through everyday life. This is best done in the struggles – that's where most of His defining, refining work is done. *Do not conform any longer to the pattern of this world, but be transformed by the renewing of your mind. Then you will be able to test and approve what God's will is – His good, pleasing and perfect will.* Romans 12:2.

I'm a planner and strongly believe in the adage "no one plans to fail, they just fail to plan." I like to make plans and enjoy when I can see progress being made on what I've planned. But sometimes I can get so caught up in my plans that God has to take drastic measures to get my attention and pull me back on course – and I don't think I'm alone in this struggle. Most of us have to lose hope in our own plans working out before we truly place hope in the plan God is trying to work out through us. When things seem to be going right, I have found we spend less time trying to discern if our right aligns with God's direction for our lives. It is in the challenges, struggles and closed doors that we'll often pause and check our direction to see if we've gotten off track. In today's culture we rely on navigation systems to get us where we want to go. But experience has shown that these systems are only as good as the information that is programed into them. Bad info in, bad info out. Who we place our trust in and choose to follow makes all the difference in where we will end up also. Only when we look to God and follow His Word can we find the path He has for us. We don't know where we're going in the big picture – but God does. He strategically gets us in the right place at the right time, to be used by Him. But we must be paying attention and listening for His voice. We must guard against becoming so self-absorbed in living our plan that we miss when God's trying to give us directions for His plan. "Only one life twill soon be past. Only what's done for Christ will last." C.T. Studd

Struggles are opportunities for change, but it's up to each of us to decide what we will do with what we've been given. Can we look for good in something that doesn't seem good? Can we use our trials, losses, deformities and diseases as opportunities for God to shine in and through us despite our loss or weakness? Charles Swindoll says, "We are all faced with a series of great opportunities brilliantly disguised as impossible situations." Our weaknesses can put God's power on display – or not. It really depends on how we handle what we've been given. How we respond to difficult times says a lot about our God – how we see Him and if we believe Him. 2 Corinthians 12:9-10 tells us how to respond to struggles, ...*Therefore I will boast all the more gladly about my weaknesses, so that Christ's power may rest on me. That is why, for Christ's sake, I delight in weaknesses, in insults, in hardships, in persecutions, in difficulties. For when I am weak, then I am strong.* I am personally challenged to delight in weaknesses and trials but we can draw comfort knowing that as long as God has us in His refining fire, we've not been tossed aside to the scrap heap. Trials do not mean we've walked out of His will, but more likely into His plan. Billy Graham reminds us, "We shouldn't think of ourselves and how weak we are. Instead we should think about God and how strong He is."

Trials do not mean we've walked out of His will, but more likely into His plan.

When our immediate interests and God's long-term goals collide, we can feel frustration: frustrated that we cannot seem to get what we want; frustrated that it is taking so long; frustrated that it appears God is not listening. Yet all this frustration can be a result of not understanding His plan. He is looking at our ultimate good, while we're focused on immediate relief and satisfaction. Frustration on our part does not hurry God on His part. We cannot push God and He won't push us. He is content to wait until we submit and learn. If we don't like the timeframe, maybe we need to become a better student. If we can learn to praise God through our challenges, and delight in hardship, persecution and difficulties, then we will ultimately be strengthened, and God will be glorified.

Questions to Ponder:

1. What do you believe is the plan God has for you in life? Are you living it yet?

2. What is your response when facing what appears to be spiritual warfare?

3. How can we allow suffering and struggles to bring God the glory during the trial, not just after it's passed?

4. In what areas of your life do you feel you sit on the fence, trying to have both worlds? What can you do to alleviate this dilemma?

APPLICATION

PREMISE SIX: What if most of my difficult challenges are not Satan trying to harm me, but God trying to shape me?

IF THIS IS TRUE, perhaps difficult times are not outside God's plan, but are part of the plan.

"Don't bear trouble, use it. Take whatever happens –justice and injustice, pleasure and pain, compliment and criticism – take it up into the purpose of your life and make something out of it. Turn it into a testimony."
–E. Stanley Jones

Forgiveness:

How can we help someone move from the struggle and everything that comes with it: hopelessness, disappointment, loss, confusion and help them see God's grander plan with endless possibilities for their future? Is it possible to take the challenges, conflicts and needs someone faces and help them find God in their life journey? Without God, all life is lived in vain. But, I think it's difficult to suggest to someone who is struggling that God has a plan and He can use these times to refine and equip them for the better life, especially if they don't know God. From my experience, it should never be done lightly, it's not done easily and most of all – it's not done enough.

Romans 8:28, *And we know that in all things God works for the good of those who love Him, who have been called according to His purpose* is a confusing verse in the face of truly devastating and cruel acts. How does one speak this verse to someone suffering from rape, abuse, molestation, murder or many other such atrocities? I think it's important to clarify that this verse does not state that all things are good. Some things are evil and they'll never, in and of themselves, become good. But if we dwell on the evil done to us, we'll also be unable to heal and move past it. That's where Romans 8:28 comes in. God can work for our good despite evil, in place of evil, beyond the evil that happened to us. Too often we stop at the tragedy, viewing all life with a perspective of how we lived before and how we stopped living after. Bringing God into the tragedy can give us hope beyond and in spite of the tragedy.

The act of forgiveness is an important piece in helping someone move past the hurt they've experienced. You might be saying, "Some things are just too big and bad to forgive." Let me clarify how I view forgiveness by explaining what I believe it is and what it isn't. Think of unforgiveness as a toxic poison that infects the person who carries it and slowly starts to steal their vigor for life. Most of the time unforgiveness is sealed tight inside the one who has been wronged, never spilling on to the one who committed the wrong. The one who ultimately suffers the most is the one who can't forgive – because when someone can't forgive, they don't move on. Whatever happened now holds them hostage. It controls and impacts what they do, how they behave and can jeopardize their hope for a fulfilled future. Someone who cannot forgive will daily relinquish power to the person who violated or hurt them.

Forgiveness is about releasing the poison, getting it out so the one who was offended can get on with life. I believe the act of forgiveness is handing the violator or the violation over to God. It is confessing to God you can't carry it anymore and He must. It's not giving in or insinuating that the violator or the act is good, it's giving it up to God so you can move on. All of us want justice served and when we've been violated and hurt, we would like to see it happen now. But life isn't fair and justice won't always come in our lifetime. Nevertheless, we do have God's promise that one day the perpetrators will face His judgment. In 2 Corinthians 5:10 we are told, *For we must all appear before the judgment seat of Christ, that each one may receive what is due him for the things done while in the body, whether good or bad.*

...the act of forgiveness is handing the violator or the violation over to God.

When a person cannot forgive, over time their lack of forgiveness begins to define them. This inability to forgive becomes a mechanism to hurt others or to make people feel sorry or guilty. Unforgiveness can deceive us by making us feel we're in control or even morally superior, but in reality, it is a sin. Matthew 6:14-15 says, *"For if you forgive men when they sin against you, your heavenly Father will also forgive you. But if you do not forgive men their sins, your Father will not forgive your sins."* Refusing to do something God has told us to do can have grave consequences for the one who chooses to be disobedient. Any sin issue we don't deal with affects our life, our future and our eternity and an inability to forgive is no different. We are sinners, saved by grace and in need of forgiveness. But I want to be really clear – encouraging someone to forgive does not mean you are suggesting they should reconcile, restore or even begin a relationship with the one who hurt them. Anyone questioning if they should have contact with their offender should be encouraged to seek counsel or even professional guidance before taking action. Sometimes healing involves communication or contact with the one who hurt them, many times it does not. Regardless, if God is going to work good out of something horrific, it cannot begin until there is forgiveness. We can help others let go and release to God what happened to them, which can then open the door to limitless possibilities moving forward.

We need to bring this truth to others who come to us with struggles that cannot be surmounted except with Christ. Our answers should not be small and pain-dulling, but powerfully healing through the only One who can work good out of tragedy. Tragedy should never be allowed to define anyone's future, but rather given over to the only true source of hope, our Lord Jesus Christ, who can take all things and work them for our good and God's glory.

Our Good and His Glory:

Entering into the struggle with others is critical if we want to help them understand God can work good out of whatever has happened. To bring clarity and offer solid, good advice we need to understand the situation. This isn't a casual one-sentence conversation, but an in-depth dialog to get a grasp of what's going on and what contributed to their current struggle. It is not just getting the inside scoop, but a chance to bring hope to their situation by expanding their vision beyond their current situation. Struggles tend to narrow our focus so all we see is the challenge. To help someone think about life beyond the struggle, conversations need to move to what they can look forward to or what they want to change in their life. This brings hope into difficult times, but also gives everyone something to focus on and plan for. In 2 Corinthians 4:16-18 we are told, *Therefore we do not lose heart. Though outwardly we are wasting away, yet inwardly we are being renewed day by day. For our light and momentary troubles are achieving for us an eternal glory that far outweighs them all. So we fix our eyes not on what is seen, but on what is unseen. For what is seen is temporary, but what is unseen is eternal.*

To truly help others we have to reverse how we view challenges, in both their life and ours. Regardless of how problems get to us, God has allowed them to pass through His hand into our life and He can use them for our good and His glory – if we allow it. Lamentations 3:37-38, *Who can speak and have it happen if the Lord has not decreed it? Is it not from the mouth of the Most High that both calamities and good things come?* God loves us but also sees our potential and is not content leaving us as we are. He doesn't leave us alone or take the easy way out by giving us what we want. He uses the struggle to further His plan, refining our potential. Given that is how God works, I personally do not think He's pleased when we find satisfaction loving people as they are, without also encouraging them to see and pursue their full potential. When we help relieve their struggle, but don't engage God in the struggle, it becomes more about us than them. Not using a struggle to leverage opportunities for life improvement makes it merely an act of compassion or pity. Acts of mercy and love that end up feeding someone in their misfortune rather than feeding into their life, fall short of what God has modeled for us to emulate. We are instructed in Proverbs 16:21, *The wise in heart are called discerning, and pleasant words promote instruction.*

Not using a struggle to leverage opportunities for life improvement makes it merely an act of compassion or pity.

Even when we have sought God and are offering our best, the outcome of our actions can have unintended consequences beyond our ability to control or predict. These unexpected consequences might result in additional drawbacks or adverse results. That is why offering compassion that is redemptive cannot be random, casual or reactive. There are times when our best attempts to help someone will seem to fail. But as Kingdom workers, we are still called to do our best with what God has given us, releasing the results into His hands. *"You intended to harm me, but God intended it for good to accomplish what is now being done, the saving of many lives."* Genesis 50:20. We don't have the big picture, only God does. We don't know how He's fitting all the pieces together. Without God, our best efforts will fall short, but with God even our disasters can be turned into victories.

Not for the Faint of Heart:

Sometimes God's plan to mature us actually means He turns up the heat, the losses are greater and the struggles more intense. We can't always discern if it's God's plan by how things are going. So how can we encourage someone to stay the course when it's unclear if they're headed in the right direction? It really comes down to a matter of focus, keeping our eyes on Jesus, who endured incredible opposition for the ultimate prize. *Let us fix our eyes on Jesus, the author and perfecter of our faith, who for the joy set before Him endured the cross, scorning its shame, and sat down at the right hand of the throne of God. Consider Him who endured such opposition from sinful men, so that you will not grow weary and lose heart.* Hebrews 12:2-3.

From all outward appearances it didn't seem like God's plan for Jesus was going well and if the effectiveness of His ministry was based on how well He was received – He should have quit. He faced strong opposition, especially from the learned scholars, leaders and those in authority. But He continued with His work, showing love, speaking truth, doing His Father's will without compromise or hesitation. In Luke 4:28-30 we read, *All the people in the synagogue were furious when they heard this. They got up, drove Him out of the town, and took Him to the brow of the hill on which the town was built, in order to throw Him down the cliff. But He walked right through the crowd and went on His way.* We do not read in the Bible conversations about it not working and Christ wondering if He should change or quit what He was doing. He didn't suggest they go a different direction or try a different message using different tactics more palatable to those who were listening. Even in Gethsemane on the eve of His arrest the account from Matthew 26:39 says, *Going a little farther, He fell with His face to the ground and prayed, "My Father, if it is possible, may this cup be taken from me. Yet not as I will, but as you will."* He was so close to His Father that He didn't surrender to discouragment, even when death was near. He just kept doing what God had sent Him to do.

How often do we, after discerning what we believe God has called us to, hesitate, question or give up when faced with opposition and criticism?

It's important to hear from God before we start, but then we should boldly move out in His will and persevere, regardless of results or opinions as we move forward. Redemptive Compassion will be met with opposition. Expect it and ignore it. Keep your eyes on the Lord and your feet on the path. This is not for the faint of heart – it's for the Kingdom warriors committed to heavenly work. Psalm 25:4-5 says, *Show me your ways, O Lord, teach me your paths; guide me in your truth and teach me, for you are God my Savior, and my hope is in you all day long.* We cannot judge success by what we see, but we can discern by what we believe God's Spirit reveals to us. Offering redemptive compassion to someone is not easy and often some of the results along the way seem to point to failure. The only way we'll stay the course is to spend sufficient time at the start discerning the course and then, through God's strength and His direction, stay committed to the end.

Questions to Ponder:

1. What do you think will be some of your challenges in suggesting that some struggles are part of God's plan to mold us, not hold us down?

2. Forgiveness is such a critical part of God being able to work in someone's life. How has it impacted your own life, either in giving it or being shown it?

3. If all things pass through God's hand into our life, do you agree they can be used for our good and His glory? Explain.

4. Do you agree that to those looking on, a lot of Jesus' three years of ministry appeared to be a failure? How should this encourage us to persevere regardless of the struggle or outward appearance that it's failing?

✳ Premise SEVEN

"We must pray as if it depends upon God and work as if it depends upon us."

–Mark Batterson

What if God wants me
to look to Him more than I look
out for myself?

Trust:

It seems like I've always had trust issues. My failing first marriage, which ultimately ended in divorce, seemed to solidify in my mind that I couldn't trust anyone. As the marriage fell apart I realized the man I had known since my teen years, wasn't the person I thought he was. I then decided you never really know anybody. You only know who they let you see and some people are experts at being who you want, but not who they are. Over the years I have continued to struggle trusting people. I realized I really needed to work on my trust issues when I found myself unwilling to go anywhere without my purse, just in case the person I was with left me. I didn't want to be stranded and I felt the only one I could really trust was myself.

I accepted God early as Lord of my life and have been in a relationship with Him for what seems most of my life. But I have trust issues with Him also. As I struggled with my health issues that were limiting my ability to do things, I found myself questioning God. Could I trust that He would take care of me if I didn't get better? Was He going to keep me in His plans and could I trust that He was not done with me, when I seemed to be a shell of the person I once was? I knew this time of healing was a season when God wanted to grow my trust. He wanted me to let go and look to Him more than I was looking out for myself, which I had become adept at doing over the years. While I falsely believed I could take care of myself, I couldn't heal my body and I had to trust God in spite of my declining health. The verses in Proverbs 3:5-6 became a source of comfort to me, *Trust in the Lord with all your heart and lean not on your own understanding; in all your ways acknowledge Him, and He will make your paths straight.*

He wanted me to let go and look to Him more than I was looking out for myself.

I wonder if Joseph struggled with trust issues? After he was sold to the Ishmaelites, they sold him to Potiphar, where Joseph prospered in his work.

Was it because he trusted God would take care of him? Then he was falsely accused by Potiphar's wife and sent to prison, yet we read in Genesis 39:20-21, *...But while Joseph was there in the prison, the Lord was with him; He showed him kindness and granted him favor in the eyes of the prison warden.* Did Joseph continue to excel because he trusted God was with him? When the chief cupbearer forgot about the promise he had made to Joseph after he was released, did Joseph continue to trust God as his circumstances deteriorated? I personally do not understand how he didn't lose hope, yet I'm convinced he didn't. When he was brought before Pharaoh and given a chance to possibly win his freedom, he continued to highlight God, not himself. How had Joseph used thirteen years of imprisonment to build trust with God? I think many of us would have had our trust diminished or crushed when our God could, but didn't, rescue us time and time again. Perhaps it was because *...He persevered because he saw Him who is invisible.* Hebrews 11:27. Maybe Joseph trusted God because he knew, without a doubt, that God was with him every step of the way.

Is God Asking Too Much?

Our natural instinct is to protect ourselves. It goes against human nature to be obedient to God when it can negatively affect us personally. God, however, is focused on turning our human nature into His divine nature, which can be humbling. We are told we can't live for applause, but we also are warned we can't stop because of criticism. Are we willing to risk all for Christ so we can live fully in Christ? As stated in Galatians 2:20, *"I have been crucified with Christ and I no longer live, but Christ lives in me."* When we pray prayers that are humanly possible for us to achieve, just in case God doesn't come through, we steal His glory. Playing it safe takes small faith and as Mark Batterson says, "If we aren't willing to risk our reputation, we'll never establish God's reputation." Prayers that glorify God are impossible for us to do without Him. Impossible prayers that align with God's will, don't put our reputation on the line – they put His reputation on the line. Impossible, God-aligned prayers are what miracles are made of!

As I read Bible stories it seems God often reduces His chosen before He uses them. As we've seen in Joseph's story, he received God's promise, only to spend most of his early adult life in prison where God refined him from an arrogant youngster to a humble and powerful man. Gideon's army was reduced to only 300 men before God sent him into the battle. David, hiding in the cave, was tested by God to see if he would forcibly take the crown or wait for God's timing. Moses, consumed by his anger for the injustice shown his people, had to flee into exile for 40 years before God called him back to service. Finally, and perhaps one of my personal favorites is Noah. Old and living in a desert, Noah was told by God to build an ark. Can you imagine the ridicule he faced from everyone around him as he spent, some estimate 50-75 years, building a boat in the middle of the desert because God told him to? In each of these examples, God brought these men to a place where, stripped of all personal aspirations, they looked to Him for everything – timing, strength and position – more than they were looking out for themselves.

Are we willing to be obedient to God even if it means we might look foolish to those who watch us? Too often we pray to reach God for our purposes rather than submit ourselves to God for His purposes. Phillips Brooks said, "Nothing lies beyond the reach of prayer except that which lies outside the will of God." Often we pray to God for answers, but we also need to pray that our prayers align with His will. I know that sometimes I want to succeed because I don't want to look foolish or fail and I realize it's more about how others view me than whether I've heard from God correctly. We must become more focused on being obedient to God and less concerned about looking foolish to those who watch.

Too often we pray to reach God for our purposes rather than submit ourselves to God for His purposes.

Perhaps we hesitate, delay or stop because we are afraid of making the wrong decision, but no decision will ever circumvent God's plan and that's a promise given to us in Proverbs 21:30, *There is no wisdom, no insight, no plan that can succeed against the Lord.* We can never mess up in such a way God cannot undo, redo or cancel completely if need be. Fear of making a wrong decision causes indecision that can paralyze. Yet believing God can right our wrongs doesn't negate spending time in prayer and waiting on the Lord before we act – in fact it should further necessitate it. But when it's time to move, slow obedience likens to disobedience. Let us step out in faith, as weak as it may seem and not give in to doubts, as strong as they may be, to do that which God asks: whatever, whenever and however He asks.

Does God seem to be asking too much from you right now and does the passion He's placed in your heart seem more hindered than empowered? Be patient and keep your eyes on your Almighty God who's grooming you for the call He's placed on your life. Sometimes His pruning shears cut deep, and new growth is difficult to identify – but don't give up or lose hope. If God has called you, wait until He calls you to step out and then move boldly and with confidence believing it will happen just as He has said. We know our faith is maturing when we embrace humility, sorrow, fear, temptations, delays or unseen answers to our prayers as necessary in our journey toward Christ-likeness. The more we mature as a Christian, the more readily we will embrace situations that make us feel immature.

Living Sacrifice:

In Romans 12:1 we are called to be living sacrifices for God; *Therefore, I urge you, brothers, in view of God's mercy, to offer your bodies as living sacrifices, holy and pleasing to God – which is your spiritual worship.* The challenge is that as a living sacrifice, we can crawl off the altar as our mood and circumstances dictate. Revelation 3:1-2 warns us, *"…I know your deeds; you have a reputation of being alive, but you are dead. Wake up! Strengthen what remains and is about to die, for I have not found your deeds complete in the sight of my God."* Bottom line – we are fickle.

Are we willing to die for Christ, but perhaps even more difficult, to live boldly for Christ? Both require sacrifice and a willingness to surrender our free will. Are we truly willing to become a living sacrifice, completely sold out to Christ? As Paul states in Philippians 1:20-21, *I eagerly expect and hope that I will in no way be ashamed, but will have sufficient courage so that now as always Christ will be exalted in my body, whether by life or by death. For to me, to live is Christ and to die is gain.* We can mouth the words and know the Scriptures, but I have personally found living for Christ to be a challenge and the temptation to crawl off the altar enticing at times.

Eli was a priest, chosen by God and living for God, but when it came to his sons he crawled off the altar. He did not restrain or keep his sons from committing grave sins against God and because of this God punished his family for generations to come. The Israelites begged God for a king, so God reluctantly granted their request and gave them Saul. Yet Saul's need to be accepted and successful cost him everything. His outward behavior, choices and appearance became more important than obeying God and in the end, he too had crawled off the altar. A disobedient living sacrifice displeases God. In 1 Samuel 15:22-23 we are told, *"...To obey is better than sacrifice, and to heed is better than the fat of rams. For rebellion is like the sin of divination, and arrogance like the evil of idolatry. Because you have rejected the word of the Lord, He has rejected you as king."* History has shown God allows His chosen ones to crawl off the altar, but not without consequences. In 1 Corinthians 10:21-22 we are warned, *You cannot drink the cup of the Lord and the cup of demons too; you cannot have a part in both the Lord's table and the table of demons. Are we trying to arouse the Lord's jealousy? Are we stronger than He?* A living sacrifice for Christ must be willing to give all God asks, when He asks.

As fellow Kingdom workers, we must abhor evil and take whatever steps are necessary to eradicate it, even if it involves family or someone God has sent us to help. God is a jealous and righteous God and He holds us accountable, not just for our sins but for the sins of those under our care. We cannot afford to tolerate sin, not in our own lives and not in the lives of those God has given us to care for. *"That servant who knows his master's will and does not get ready or does not do what his master wants will be beaten with many blows...From everyone who has been given much, much will be demanded; and from the one who has been entrusted with much, much more will be asked."* Luke 12:47-48

All of us need to examine ourselves to see if sin has taken up residency in some private place in our mind or soul. Perhaps we are not the person we show when in the public eye, putting forth our best for all to see. Let us never pretend to be someone we're not. Let us guard against making good decisions in public, but poor decisions in our private life. If we don't have integrity when only God is watching, we'll eventually run out of the fake integrity we put on display in public. If we want to know the real condition of our heart, we should reflect on who we are in private: what we do, think and how we behave when we're by ourselves or with our immediate family. Who that person is best reveals our true identity. "The strength of a man's virtue must not be measured by his efforts, but by his ordinary life." Pascal.

Any sin endured and not eradicated, at some point will be embraced.

Any sin endured and not eradicated, at some point will be embraced. Sin in small doses dulls us into complacency. Complacency leads to apathy and that leads to normalcy. That which should repulse us, will eventually not affect us as we become dulled, tolerating something that should be intolerable. James 1:14-15 warns us, *But each one is tempted when, by his own evil desire, he is dragged away and enticed. Then, after desire has conceived, it gives birth to sin; and sin, when it is full-grown, gives birth to death.* If we earnestly seek truth, God will show us if we've crawled off the altar, unwilling to sacrifice something or someone in our life. *Search me, O God, and know my heart; test me and know my anxious thoughts. See if there is any offensive way in me, and lead me in the way everlasting.* Psalm 139:23-24.

When we fail, the enemy will try to convince us it's over, there's no turning back, condemning us to a life of hell. On the other hand, once we realize we've gone astray, a prayer prayed in earnest, will allow the Holy Spirit to convict us and help us find our way back to God. There is a great difference between conviction and condemnation. The Spirit, if allowed, convicts to change us. Satan, when allowed, uses guilt to condemn. One moves us forward, the other holds us captive in our sin. We are not destitute if we've crawled or fallen off the altar of our Lord. As a living sacrifice there is always hope in Christ that we can crawl back on, but it's up to us. God waits, but He does not interfere, until we ask Him to help us find our way back home.

Questions to Ponder:

1. Describe your level of trust and what has influenced it over the years.
2. Have you thought of yourself as a living sacrifice for God? What entices you to crawl off the altar?
3. The Holy Spirit convicts, Satan condemns. In your own words explain the difference between conviction and condemnation.

APPLICATION

PREMISE SEVEN: What if God wants me to look to Him more than I look out for myself?

IF THIS IS TRUE, we will have to sacrifice our own self-image to bear His image.

"Every human being is an image-bearer of God."
–Ray Vander Laan

Training for Kingdom Work:

One of my favorite quotes comes from Dallas Willard who said, "We cannot continue to try to do Kingdom work, we must train to do Kingdom work." Most helping efforts are done out of ignorance, driven by passion and a misplaced compassion. God's Word is filled with how to help, yet we latch onto those few passages most of us know, that make us feel good, but do not require too much from us. Churches spend money and time educating those who attend their church on how to evangelize effectively, pray powerfully, worship uninhibitedly and disciple others – all good things. But when was the last time you were in a church that offered a course on how to offer biblical, wholistic help? It puzzles me that so little is taught on something every church feels biblically called to do. Most church people who have a desire to do a ministry of assistance are ill-equipped for what they will face. We would never send someone into battle without appropriate training or weapons, but think nothing about sending Kingdom workers into the battle of need with little more than a heart of compassion. I believe it's time to study how God has called us to do redemptive work and once learned, implement it regardless of how hard it is. We are told in James 1:22-25, *Do not merely listen to the word, and so deceive yourselves. Do what it says. Anyone who listens to the word but does not do what it says is like a man who looks at his face in a mirror and, after looking at himself, goes away and immediately forgets what he looks like. But the man who looks intently into the perfect law that gives freedom, and continues to do this, not forgetting what he has heard, but doing it – he will be blessed in what he does.*

Radical love asks us to walk a narrow road of self-denial, but in our present-day culture we are told to watch out for ourselves and how we're treated. Growing up in Christ should be about what is happening within us, not to us, as we strive to be His hands and feet. Too often we pay great attention to how others behave and respond in like manner, giving people what they want, often at the expense of what they need. A selfless, Christ-centered love can do what is right even when it doesn't feel right, focused more on the long-term outcome than any temporary relief. We should expect the secular world to do what feels good and is easily counted, but I find that Christians are equally drawn to relief and recovery, much more than redemption and restoration. We are excited to help in ways that feel fulfilling and find it exhilarating when God allows us to be part of Kingdom work that seems to be working. But when God asks us to do things which don't make earthly sense and actually seem like the wrong thing to do, we find it hard to be part of the plan. If what we are doing, using seemingly ineffective methods, seems wrong, naive or a waste of time, our pride can get in the way. We all want to win for Christ and do successful things, but sometimes God needs us to do something that actually appears to be losing at the moment because there is a bigger plan that only God can know. I've heard it said we see life from the first story, but God has the upper story view. He sees not just what is in front of us, but what's to come with the full picture in mind. Sometimes what seems like an immediate loss, will take the most ground for Christ in the future.

It is a huge responsibility to be in a position of influence over another person.

It is a huge responsibility to be in a position of influence over another person. Perhaps that is one reason many are drawn to give stuff more than give of themselves. Perhaps we subconsciously think we can do less harm in the giving of things. But giving things that offer temporary help that enable people to continue living beneath their potential makes them a prisoner of their situation, dependent on others for survival. Walking through challenges with someone is never something we should do lightly. We need to prepare ourselves privately before God before we attempt to walk publicly with others. *If anyone speaks, he should do it as one speaking the very words of God. If anyone serves, he should do it with the strength God provides, so that in all things God may be praised through Jesus Christ. To Him be the glory and power forever and ever. Amen.* 1 Peter 4:11.

No Guarantees:

As we learn to sacrifice our own self-image to bear His image, we will care less about what others think as our confidence in who we are in Christ grows. This confidence should help us respond appropriately to those we help without fearing criticism. Redemptive helping efforts will often be contrary to the ways of the world and we should expect to face criticism and skepticism from those who do not understand biblical, wholistic help. In fact, in my opinion, if we're more concerned about how our actions look to others over making sure we're helping people wholistically, people would be better off without our help. Redemptive compassion means we focus on what God has told us to do even if it appears ridiculous, unloving or unwise to those watching. To stand boldly for Christ means we should expect to be chastised and criticized, as told in 2 Timothy 3:12, *In fact, everyone who wants to live a godly life in Christ Jesus will be persecuted.*

Because His ways are not our ways, His timing matters. Knowing when to come or go because we believe God has said, "now go, I am with you," is important. Man will push us, tell us what the right thing is and when we are to do this right thing – but let us not be deceived. Nonbelievers are blinded to God's ways, they don't have His wisdom or any understanding of His methods. In 1 Corinthians 1:18-19 we are told, *For the message of the cross is foolishness to those who are perishing, but to us who are being saved it is the power of God. For it is written: "I will destroy the wisdom of the wise; the intelligence of the intelligent I will frustrate."* Unless God has said now is the time and this is the thing to do – we need to continue to wait in prayer. When Jesus' own family tried to push Him to go to the Feast He replied, *"You go the Feast. I am not yet going up to this Feast, because for me the right time has not yet come."* John 7:8. Jesus was close enough to God that He knew exactly when to go and when to stay. How much more effective could we be if we became better at discerning and hearing God's voice, in spite of the crowd yelling and pushing us around?

To stand boldly for Christ means we should expect to be chastised and criticized.

I have found it's hard to live boldly for God and play it safe at the same time. God asks us to be obedient and submissive, but not necessarily safe. Mark

Batterson says, "We can't afford to live as if our purpose in life is to arrive safely at death." Scripture talks a lot about living boldly, having courage, persevering, but safe – not much that I can find. If we wait for the assurance that what we do will succeed we could miss out playing our part. Francis Chan says, "God doesn't call us to be comfortable. He calls us to trust Him so completely that we are unafraid to put ourselves in situations where we will be in trouble if He doesn't come through." When God sends us out He wants us to do all we can, with what we've been given, not asking or expecting success in worldly terms. We can't hold back, waiting for guaranteed success, but must be willing to take calculated risks when Spirit led. After Moses died, God gave Joshua some very specific instructions for entering the Promised Land found in Joshua 1:9 *"Have I not commanded you? Be strong and courageous. Do not be terrified; do not be discouraged, for the Lord your God will be with you wherever you go."* Mature Kingdom workers seek the Lord and are willing to do whatever God opens before them. They understand that Kingdom success looks differently than worldly success. *Sow your seed in the morning, and at evening let not your hands be idle, for you do not know which will succeed, whether this or that, or whether both will do equally well.* Ecclesiastes 11:6. It should not matter if it appears to man that we have failed when we know in our heart that we have been faithful in our work. Craig Groeschel says, "To step toward your destiny, you might have to leave your security." We don't need worldly success to advance Kingdom work. God often flips things upside down to accomplish His greater purposes and James 1:9-10 says, *The brother in humble circumstances ought to take pride in his high position. But the one who is rich should take pride in his low position, because he will pass away like a wild flower.*

Rick Warren says, "You don't have to compromise convictions to be compassionate," yet I see Christians struggle with this all the time. For some reason we've become confused and have forgotten the main reason we do Kingdom work is to bear His image and bring His message to those we serve and those who watch. When we compromise convictions we don't resemble Christ. We are not to seek peace at any cost! In Matthew 10:34 Jesus states very clearly, *"Do not suppose that I have come to bring peace to the earth. I did not come to bring peace, but a sword."* Too often we are so focused on pleasing and appeasing that we bear little resemblance to our Savior. His death conquered sin and when our helping efforts allow people to remain trapped and living in bondage to their need, that very bondage Jesus died to release us from, we have not been His image-bearer, but have raised up our own form of saviorhood! *It is for freedom that Christ has set us free. Stand firm, then, and do not let yourselves be burdened again by a yoke of slavery.* Galatians 5:1. What is the ultimate purpose of responding to need? Is it to highlight ourselves or God? As Kingdom workers about our Father's business, at the end of each day we should ask ourselves, "How well did I put God on display as I lived out this day?" Our answer will tell us much about how well we sacrificed our own self-image to bear His image.

Questions to Ponder:

1. Have you studied or trained how to offer biblical, wholistic help? Why or why not?

2. Do you agree that we might have to sacrifice our own self-image to bear Christ's image? Explain.

3. If you agree we don't have to compromise convictions to be compassionate, why do we often compromise in order to appear more compassionate?

✳ Premise EIGHT

"You will be graced with the disaster your soul requires to find its way home."

–Tim Farrington

What if God wants to
be enough and will allow or use
whatever it takes to
get me to understand this?

Is God Enough?

I can still remember the day like it was yesterday. It was week five in recovery from the second surgery and my "come to Jesus" meeting with God. Two more surgeries lay in front of me and I was questioning my road to recovery with this one. While confined to sitting I had earnestly sought God, but had only received disjointed thoughts that seemed unrelated. I chuckle now knowing you are reading these jumbled, scrambled thoughts, but back to my story. As I sat quietly the first question bubbled inside me as my spirit felt God's probing, "Lois, am I enough if you don't recover fully from any of these surgeries? Am I enough?" The next one cascaded quickly on top of the first, "Lois, am I enough if you can't return to the work I know is so important to you? Am I enough?" By now, questions were flowing through me as tears flowed from me. "Am I enough if I never give you more to write? Am I enough if you can't take care of your yard or your house? Am I enough if you can't go on walks or go camping or any of those things that please you? Lois, am I enough?" I have to admit, while I wanted Him to be enough, at that moment in my life, He wasn't. I wanted to go back to the work I loved, the writing that gave me purpose and to have full health that allowed me to live the lifestyle I had grown to love. I wanted more. As I sat and contemplated the questions, I realized God needed me to get to the place where He was enough. He needed me to let go of everything I was fighting so hard to preserve and give it to Him. Feeling totally broken, I earnestly and fervently made a soul decision that day, committing, with His help to make Him enough. From that day forward I have worked on building trust and looking for ways to praise Him no matter what. It hasn't been easy. I still struggle at times. But it was a life-changing, forever-freeing moment for me. I can now say with confidence, "My God is enough and I will choose to trust Him with my future."

Joseph, on the other hand, seemed to have come to terms with this question quickly. Someday, I hope I run into Joseph in heaven so I can ask Him if he ever struggled with some of the same things I have. If I was to take a guess though, from my limited knowledge in reading the Scriptures, I think Joseph surrendered to God early so no matter how often his life situation changed, he knew God was enough. As I read his story, Joseph, not knowing if this was all life had for him, still seemed to excel, advance and hold prominent positions in very unlikely places. It's as if knowing that his God was enough freed him to do all things well and to be used by God in powerful ways that eventually changed the course of history. Once we determine God is enough, we can replace the fear of what we might lose with confidence in what God can do. Joseph proved that he was a free man in God, regardless of the chains and restrictions placed on him. That was all he needed to succeed.

Worshiping the Blessing:

We are a blessed people. God has given us much to enjoy and Psalm 37:4 says, *Delight yourself in the Lord and He will give you the desires of your heart.* I think all of us love the promise in this verse, but often overlook the *delight yourself in the Lord* part. If our blessings get in the way of delighting in Him, do we begin to worship His blessings rather than build our relationship with Him? If God strips us of our health, family, work and other blessings, are we still be able to delight in Him? We cannot fully live to Christ until we die to self. I have personally experienced God using whatever means necessary to put things in their proper order, including taking the blessings He's bestowed on me, when they got in the way.

We cannot fully live to Christ until we die to self.

To truly be a Christ-follower we should not be afraid of being stripped of our possessions, popularity or position if that is what God chooses to do. The cost of following Christ is great and at some point we will be required to lose something we've let get in front of God. What we lose may seem great at the time, but the gain is even greater. Perhaps God may not grant us success in order to determine our loyalty. He may choose to take our possessions to evaluate our heart. We may lose a position we're proud of and have worked hard at, so He can get our attention. In Psalm 135:6 we are told, *The Lord does whatever pleases Him, in the heavens and on the earth, in the seas and all their depths.* God is willing to go to whatever lengths necessary to bring us back into a right relationship with Him. He's willing to use great adversity to get our attention or re-ignite a conscience that has grown dull and lethargic. If we've learned to ignore His small signals, He does not hesitate to use a larger signal to shock us into sensing His presence. If our pain throws us on our knees and into His arms, so be it. He is unrelenting in His pursuit of our soul. We are told to seek the Kingdom of God first...if wooing us doesn't do it, perhaps pain will! "God whispers to us in our pleasures, speaks to us in our conscience, but shouts to us in our pain; it is His megaphone to a deaf world." C.S. Lewis.

No matter what we have or lack, what He gives or removes, what He brings to life or lets die, God wants us to learn *He is enough.* At some point in our life each of us will face trials and difficulties that force us to move out of public service and into private suffering for a period of time. Paul faced those times and wrote encouragement to us in Philippians 4:10-13, *I rejoice greatly in the Lord that at last you have renewed your concern for me. Indeed, you have been concerned, but you had no opportunity to show it. I am not saying this because I am in need, for I have learned to be content whatever the circumstances. I know what it is to be in need, and I know what it is to have plenty. I have learned the secret of being content in any and every situation, whether well fed or hungry, whether living in plenty or in want. I can do everything through Him who gives me strength.* How much we have to lose to learn this lesson will be influenced by how quickly we learn. Yet I also believe that some of God's most precious, devoted followers faced incredible hardships not due to any fault of their own. Take Job for example. God allowed Satan to test Job because God was confident Job could pass the test and forty-two chapters later we see that Job didn't just pass the test, he finished well. After losing everything, literally everything, in Job chapter 42:2,5 we see him reply to the Lord, *"I know that you can do all things; no plan of yours can be thwarted. My ears had heard of you but now my eyes have seen you."* He didn't just know *of* God, he *knew* God and had found Him to be enough. If you find yourself in a difficult season I've listed a couple other verses found in Job worth reading. They can help any of us struggling through our own journey as we search to discover if God is enough. From Job 1:21 we read, ...*"Naked I came from my mother's womb, and naked I will depart. The Lord gave and the Lord has taken away; may the name of the Lord be praised."*

From Job 2:10 we read, "*...Shall we accept good from God, and not trouble?"*... Let us strive to get to the same place as Job, where we can also say with confidence, "I have seen God with my eyes and know He is enough."

Desert Times:

In Matthew 7:14 we are told, *"But small is the gate and narrow the road that leads to life, and only a few find it."* Too often, only a few find it because it forces us to leave the crowds and travel on roads not only less traveled, but often unknown and sometimes perilous. We seem to struggle learning God's sufficiency as long as there are others around us willing to meet our needs. God may have to remove us, so He can prepare us to be used by Him. This is often done in what I call the desert seasons of our lives. I live in a high plains desert so I can relate to why these dry, quiet seasons are called desert times. In the desert there is no lush foliage or abundance of water. Most things struggle to grow and what can survive the harsh conditions has adapted to the climate, with deep roots and diminished need of shade or moisture to survive. When God sends us to the desert it is often to remove us from those things that comfort us but keep our faith shallow. In the desert we are forced to send our roots down deep as God diminishes our resources and we have to look to Him for our survival.

Not everything can thrive, or even survive, in the desert times of life. It is one of the ways God gets rid of those things that are interfering in His plans for us. If you've not allowed the testing of God or resisted and fought against these desert times, you have stunted your spiritual growth. The desert times are testing times and we need to lean into them, not resist or try to escape. God wants to grow us through them, not remove us from them. If we should find an escape, we can expect to be brought back to the same lesson another time. Part of what God does in desert seasons is to help us understand our weaknesses and strengths so we will be less likely to confuse the two. God can strengthen us in our weakness, but any strength not surrendered to God, will eventually become a weakness, and we'll be tempted to move out of His will and forward in what we can do. When we step out on our own, God will let us go until we run out of our own abilities and then, when we cry out in despair, He'll pull us back into a desert time and resume His teaching.

Desert times can make us anxious. Anxiety produces tension, tension erodes joy and the loss of joy results in weakness of spirit and a victory unclaimed. We cannot move in the strength of the Lord if we carry fear and worry around in our hearts, because those emotions push out joy. In Nehemiah 8:10 we are told, *"...Do not grieve, for the joy of the Lord is your strength."* We must daily, moment by moment, choose Christ over all else and claim His promises as it states in Hebrews 12:1, *Therefore, since we are surrounded by such a great cloud of witnesses, let us throw off everything that hinders and the sin that so easily entangles, and let us run with perseverance the race marked out for us.*

Difficulties and drudgeries of desert life can make us wonder if we're alone, yet nothing could be further from the truth. God promises to always be with us and we are reminded in Hebrews 13:5, ...*"Never will I leave you; never will I forsake you."* We get our best glimpses of God when all earthly joy seems to cease. When we're stripped of everything that makes us feel good, we finally must choose if we believe God is good. Desert times are seasons of stripping us down until it seems all we have left is God – and then we realize He is all we need. Anytime we are afraid of losing something, it has some form of control over us that can drive our focus and subsequent actions. But when we lose those things, we can find ourselves being freed from what used to overwhelm, frighten or restrict us. When we get to the place where we have nothing left to lose, then there is also nothing left to fear but God Himself. This freedom can make us into a very powerfully free, Spirit-filled person. Paul states it well in Philippians 3:7-8, *But whatever was to my profit I now consider loss for the sake of Christ. What is more, I consider everything a loss compared to the surpassing greatness of knowing Christ Jesus my Lord, for whose sake I have lost all things. I consider them rubbish, that I may gain Christ.* As Janice Jo-

When we're stripped of everything that makes us feel good, we finally must choose if we believe God is good.

plin said in one of her songs, "Freedom's just another word for nothing left to lose." Finding God to be enough is the most freeing thing we can ever receive and once we've found it, nothing can hold us hostage again.

Do you know someone who has great faith? If you get to know them intimately I suspect you will find they have experienced great trials and often traveled alone, with only God's comfort, for extended periods of time in the desert. They have endured much to get to where they are today. They have learned to trust when all seems utterly hopeless; to see God, when all evidence of God is absent; to persevere when their own strength is gone; to believe when there is no visible, viable reason to believe. I am reminded of a story I heard once that impacted me: "Three women were praying as Jesus passed by. As He approached the first woman, He stopped, lovingly touched her shoulder and lingered a moment with her. When He came to the second woman, He did not pause, but gently touched her shoulder as He passed on by. As He came to the third woman, He walked quickly, with hardly a glance and no noticeable touch. Observing this I said to Him, 'Your love for the first woman was so obvious, she must have great faith, but what did the third woman do to have fallen from your grace?' This is what He said. 'The first woman is new in her faith, discourages quickly and needs constant reminders and awareness of my presence to continue in her faith. The second woman is maturing in her faith and needs less assurance to keep on her faith journey. But the third woman, ah, the third woman. She has traveled long and close with me. She knows I travel with her and does not need constant assurance of my love to continue on her faith journey. She is the one who has great faith.'" Those who have great faith have usually been greatly tested. They may have been broken, lonely, fearful and perhaps have lost almost everything but their faith, and that's when they found faith was enough. People with great faith are not necessarily people who have done great things, but are people who have experienced the greatness of their God and are a witness to those around them. Do you want great faith? Then you must be willing to suffer and grow through great trials.

Questions to Ponder:

1. Reflect on a season in your life when you faced the question, "Is God enough?"

2. How can our blessings become a stumbling block when they get in front of God?

3. Reflect on a time when you were moved out of public service and into private suffering and list some of the lessons you learned during it.

4. Do you agree that when stripped of everything, with nothing left to lose, we can become a powerfully, free person who can live and do things we might not have attempted before? Explain what this means to you in this context.

APPLICATION

PREMISE EIGHT: What if God wants to be enough and will allow or use whatever it takes to get me to understand this?

IF THIS IS TRUE, we must guard against getting in the way or in between what God is doing in the life of someone else.

"God becomes a reality when he becomes a necessity."
–Richard Foster

The Upper Story View:

God is not asking us to trust Him for a pleasant and prosperous earthly life – because that has never been His plan. We are to trust that He is enough when life is far from pleasant or prosperous. Redemptive love says we will seek the well-being of another. If the path includes suffering, love must allow it, trusting God never allows more suffering than what is truly necessary to bring someone to the good He has for them. Cynthia Mann said, "I loved them enough to give them pain, if by so doing, they might grow up good and true and beautiful in the sight of God." Can we too learn to love others enough that we will allow the trial or pain, without interference, if the end result moves them closer to God and they become stronger because of it? Our need to save others is more about us than God. We too often don't ask God what we should do before we react, leaving those we helped living in the exact same circumstances they came to us in. We need to not be afraid to let go so they can grow in God's presence.

Random, thoughtless acts of compassion can compromise the greater plan God is trying to work out in someone's life. When our helping efforts diminish God, they interrupt or circumvent whatever He is doing. We cannot be the final answer – God is. When our help doesn't include God but saves someone from their situation it can ultimately rob them of learning to know and trust their Savior. To get between someone and God hurts more than helps. C.S. Lewis said, "Kindness cares not whether its object becomes good or bad, provided only that it escapes suffering." In contrast, God's holy love cares for the whole person, not just the momentary preferences of the person. God uses all means necessary to eradicate what He finds offensive so He can move us and others toward wholeness of life. When our love action does not draw people into Christ's presence, then we have provided them an escape from the only real answer worth receiving. We have gotten between them and Christ.

It is arrogance that allows us to think we might know what is best for someone else. It is ignorance that cries out to God to lift the trial because it is too much, as if we know what is best and needed in someone's life. In Isaiah 45:11 are these strong words, *"This is what the Lord says – the Holy One of Israel, and its Maker: Concerning things to come, do you question me about my children, or give me orders about the work of my hands?"* If we believe God knows what He is doing shouldn't we trust Him even if we don't understand; even if His answers seem wrong or appear unloving? When the detachment of soldiers came to arrest Jesus we read in John 18:10 how Peter tried to defend Him, *Then Simon Peter, who had a sword, drew it and struck the high priest's servant, cutting off his right ear. (The servant's name was Malchus.)* Then we read Jesus' response in verse 11, *Jesus commanded Peter, "Put your sword away! Shall I not drink the cup the Father has given me?"* Peter, like us, had a lower-story perspective while Jesus saw from the upper story and what God needed to do to accomplish His plan. Mark Batterson says, "Our biggest problem is our small view of God. That is the cause of all lessor evils. And a high view of God is the solution to all other problems." The lower-story view is focused on relief. The upper-story view is focused on accomplishing long-term purposes that are filtered through God's Sovereignty and reveal His redemptive, restorative work. All movement starts in heaven and moves down, but we tend to view life as if everything starts on earth and moves toward heaven. Are our problems bigger than God, or is our God bigger than our problems? The more time we spend with God the more we will understand as He gives insight and discernment from "His upper-story" view.

...there is a great difference between interceding for someone and interfering in what God is doing in someone's life.

That does not mean we shouldn't pray for God's intervention, healing touch or provision. We should always offer intercessory prayer for others, but there is a great difference between interceding for someone and interfering in what God is doing in someone's life. We are told in James 5:16, *...The prayer of a righteous man is powerful and effective.* But in Matthew 16:23 we see Jesus warns Peter, "*...Out of my sight, Satan! You are a stumbling*

block to me; you do not have in mind the things of God, but the things of men." Too often we force our preferences and opinions on others as if they are God-given revelations, almost as if to say, "If I can't be God, I'll act like I'm God to my neighbor." But we are not God and we don't know what God is doing in someone's life. Isaiah 55:8-9 says, *"'For my thoughts are not your thoughts, neither are your ways my ways," declares the Lord. "As the heavens are higher than the earth, so are my ways higher than your ways and my thought than your thoughts."* Until we know what God wants us to do the best thing we can do is continue to pray and wait for Him to lead.

I Must Do Something!

I think the pressure to do something is often a contributing factor in how we respond to need. We have to do something, that's what Scripture says – or does it? Perhaps it's others who are saying we have do something and we need to do it now. I think we've all heard the statement "Don't just stand there, do something!" But I think God turns that statement around to, "Don't just do something, stand there and wait for me to instruct you in the right thing to do." Even Moses, when pressed by the Israelites for an answer in Numbers 9:8 said, ...*"Wait until I find out what the Lord commands concerning you."* Doing the right thing, at the right time, in the right way is critical in Kingdom work. When we're unsure of the next step, or any step, we need to wait for Him to direct us. Standing and waiting takes more strength and control than just reacting and doing something, anything. I think some of our need to do something immediately is because it bothers us until we do. The reality is most of us are motivated do something so we can get it off our mind and move on. I hear way too often, "I'll just do what I can and let God work it out. I'm not responsible for what they do with what I've given them, it's between them and God." I couldn't disagree more. I think that statement is a cop-out, justifying rash decisions to rush into action, while relieving themselves of all responsibility for what happens next. Proverbs 14:8 states, *The wisdom of the prudent is to give thought to their ways, but the folly of fools is deception.* I've also had someone tell me that making decisions about how to respond or putting requirements or restrictions around the need, puts us in a place of judgment and God has told us not to judge. I agree we should not judge the person in need, but we must be wise and discerning when it comes to our own actions toward the need. God will hold us accountable for what we do while in the body, good and bad and He will judge our heart behind our actions. *For God will bring every deed into judgment, including every hidden thing, whether it is good or evil.* Ecclesiastes 12:14. God watches how we love in the name of Jesus. In Matthew 7:21-23 we read strong words from Jesus, *"Not everyone who says to me, 'Lord, Lord,' will enter the kingdom of heaven, but only he who does the will of my Father who is in heaven. Many will say to me on that day, 'Lord, Lord, did we not prophesy in your name, and in your name drive out demons and perform many miracles?' Then I will tell them plainly, 'I never knew you. Away from me, you evildoers!'"*

On the flip side of reacting, we can waste an incredible amount of time trying to be sure we have correctly discerned God's will, to the point of becoming paralyzed to step out in faith when it's time. This creates unbelievable pressure, to say nothing about a prideful spirit that entertains the thought that we can figure out God's plan if we try hard enough or wait long enough. I believe the way we move in His will is to pray *first* and continually, then humbly accept and move in the direction He opens before us, leaving the closed doors alone and giving glory to Him in every deed we do. I have personally always had something I can do through a door God has opened. The problem is that it may not be what I feel pressured to do at the moment. Waiting for God and moving as He guides takes much more maturity than proceeding forward in our own strength.

> Compassion that has redemptive power cannot be done without God.

Compassion that has redemptive power cannot be done without God and if we try in our own strength we may damage more than restore. When God is working in someone's life they are often broken and fragile. If we want to touch the fragile things in people's lives we first have to see them through His eyes. We can't try to possess or control them by the methods we employ. Someone's fragility and brokenness shouldn't make us feel strong as we try to exercise some type of control over them, bargaining or debating how we'll help. When God brings someone to us, let us humbly and with caution, move gently as we try to not break their spirit, but understand what God wants us to do. We are to join God in His work, not take over to do our work. Romans 15:1-2 says, *We who are strong ought to bear with the failings of the weak and not to please ourselves. Each of us should please his neighbor for his good, to build him up.* God gives us opportunity to work in someone's life by allowing them into our life, but they are His, not ours. Let us hold loosely those things which are not ours to hold and seek to see with God's eyes, hear with His ears and feel with His heart - then and only then can we reach out and touch others as God would want us to.

Questions to Ponder:

1. Do you agree that if the path to redemption includes suffering we must allow it? Explain.

2. How can we offer intercessory prayer for someone without interfering in what we see going on?

3. Have you ever felt the need to do something, even if you didn't know if it was the right thing? Explain.

⁂ Premise NINE

"Being, not wanting, doing or having is the essence of a Spiritual life."

-Evelyn Underhill

What if God is more focused on developing my relationship with Him than on what I can do for Him?

A Human Doer:

I'm a doer and I've always been a doer. I think it's part of how God crafted me. My mother said my first words were "me do it." All my life I've not only enjoyed work, I have thrived on accomplishing tasks and doing a job well. So you can just imagine my frustration when I found myself sitting once again in recovery mode. I had already sat earlier in the year recovering from my first surgery, which by now we knew had not fixed the problem and I had another one to face in my near future. Here I was sitting again and I have to confess, not very well. I thought surely the doctor had given me extra precautions. Surely I could at least go for a drive, get out of the house or do something? Needless to say that little venture set my healing back and positioned me firmly back in the chair. I've already moaned to you how I couldn't sense God with me, probably because if I had, I would have figured out some way to write from my chair. I was truly not doing anything and the only thing I'd been given to do – sit – I was failing at miserably. It was during this sitting time I realized how much I found my purpose and worth in what I do. When doing was taken from me, I fought against emotionally feeling useless. Unable to do anything, I realized that in my Christian walk I have always struggled with the urge to try and earn my salvation which Romans 9:16 makes very clear is not possible, *It does not, therefore, depend on man's desire or effort, but on God's mercy.* I know grace is a gift and not because of anything I have done or can ever do, but that didn't seem to nullify my need to prove my worth and make my Heavenly Father proud. I found it hard to imagine God could delight in me if I wasn't accomplishing something for Him. But I was wrong. Scriptures are filled with proclamations of His love for us. One of my favorites is found in Psalm 139:17-18, *How precious to me are your thoughts, O God! How vast is the sum of them! Were I to count them, they would outnumber the grains of sand....* That's a lot of thoughts! Those six weeks taught me a lot about myself and my relationship with God as I settled in to enjoy and trust that just *being* with Him was enough!

Joseph must have placed his *relationship* with God first and what he *did* second. He learned early on to delight in the Lord, successfully accomplishing great things in any scenario he found himself in. Over and over again

Scripture says, *The Lord was with him*. The relationship was put to the test when Pharaoh, the king, had two dreams no one could interpret. The chief cupbearer, finally remembering that Joseph had interpreted his own dream while in prison, suggested him. Joseph, filled with the presence of the Lord, was not only able to interpret the dreams, but could also give Godly counsel to Pharaoh once the dreams were revealed. Joseph's boldness and confidence came from the deep relationship he had with His God who had never failed him. Joseph was a human *being* in the presence of his Lord who was just about to become one of the most influential *doers* in the Bible. He was finally ready for the assignment he had spent the last thirteen years training for. He was ready and God was with him. Together they would save the nation.

With *You* I'm Pleased:

Early in the book of Mark, God sheds light on what pleases Him. Mark 1:9-11 says, *At that time Jesus came from Nazareth in Galilee and was baptized by John in the Jordan. As Jesus was coming up out of the water, He saw heaven being torn open and the Spirit descending on Him like a dove. And a voice came from heaven: "You are my Son, whom I love; with you I am well pleased."* God was pleased with Jesus *before* He began His ministry work. As humans, we struggle to accept that God loves us for who we are and not for what we do for Him. I know it's a hard concept for me to truly grasp. Many of us tend to think what we do and how we contribute either increases or decreases our value to Him. As people who help others, it's important we understand how God sees us and the relationship He wants with us. Otherwise we'll be driven to prove our worth through performance and expect performance from others to validate their worth.

Sometimes I think we care more about what we do for God than what God wants to do in us. This can reveal underlying, selfish motives. One behavior is about doing, being busy and producing something we can feel somewhat in control of. The other is about submission and obedience, something we often feel totally out of control with. Usually what God wants to do in us is more difficult to endure than doing something that produces visible results. Billy Graham said, "You will never understand who you are until you understand who God is." The quantity of time spent with God directly impacts the quality and effectiveness of the Kingdom work we engage in. God usually won't work through us until we allow Him to complete His work in us. If the spiritual depth of our walk with others is directly correlated to the intensity of our private time with God, many of us walk crippled. There is no microwaveable version of God-time. If we want to know Him then we must first do the hard work of being in His presence. Until we're willing to get alone privately with God, I don't think we should speak or act publicly before man, especially if we're trying to lead or mentor others. How can we lead in God's ways if we've not learned God's ways because we don't know Him intimately?

God's deep truths are revealed in the quiet times, the solitary times. Too often we speak from second-hand experiences and relate what we've been told, but have not personally experienced. We know of God, but we don't know God. Who is the better teacher for how to bake a pie; someone who's only read the recipe or someone who has baked lots of pies? We can all talk a good talk, but only those who have first-hand experiences can really walk the talk. Even Elijah, God's servant, who performed powerful miracles in God's name, had moments when he doubted and as instructed in Psalm 46:10 had to, *"Be still, and know that I am God…."* In 1 Kings 19:11-13 we read how God spoke to Elijah, *…Then a great and powerful wind tore the mountains apart and shattered the rocks before the Lord, but the Lord was not in the wind. After the wind there was an earthquake, but the Lord was not in the earthquake. After the earthquake came a fire, but the Lord was not in the fire. And after the fire came a gentle whisper. When Elijah heard it, he pulled his cloak over his face and went out and stood at the mouth of the cave….* God came to Elijah in the whisper, just like He so often does with us. I don't believe God usually communicates in the crowds or in a flurry of activity. His presence goes with us, but He waits until we pull away, without worldly distractions, to speak into us. Jesus, the Son of God, who was without sin, displayed His great need of spending solitary time with His Father, going often to quiet places to pray. Matthew 14:23 is

There is no microwaveable version of God-time.

just one of many such examples, *After He had dismissed them, He went up into the hills by Himself to pray….* If Jesus couldn't do His work without continually refueling with God, how do any of us think we can do Kingdom work without doing the same? I have found it is in these quiet times, these deep times with God, that He often reveals the deep things to me. Isaiah 45:3 says, *"I will give you the treasures of darkness, riches stored in secret places, so that you may know that I am the Lord…who calls you by name."* If you want to know the deep things of God, you first must have a deep relationship with God, and out of that relationship everything else will flow.

Polluted Love:

God desires to be in relationship with us and I believe He experiences a sense of longing for us. Otherwise, why would He have sent Jesus to die for us making it possible for us to spend eternity with Him? Why would Jesus be preparing a place for us if He didn't want to be with us? In John 14:2-3 we are told, *"In my Father's house are many rooms; if it were not so, I would have told you. I am going there to prepare a place for you. And if I go and prepare a place for you, I will come back and take you to be with me that you also may be where I am."* The Bible is a love story from start to finish – from being wonderfully created in His image to the final promise of one day returning to Him. In between He woos and searches for us, corrects and disciplines in His effort to draw us back to Him. There is nothing mandated or forced about God's love. He wants us, but He wants us to want Him – to choose Him. Nothing can satisfy the longing in our soul but God. He created us and created this place within us that only He can fill. But most of us spend our whole life stuffing things and activities into this space trying to fill the void. God wants our activities and actions to be motivated by our love for Him more than our love of a cause we're committed to. This may require us to lay down our own agendas so we can join Him in the plans He has laid out. It's challenging to let go and join Him in His plan when so much of our identity is tied up in our plans.

Our love for Christ should be what motivates our service to others, but I think many of us are drawn to the emotional high we feel when we serve others. It is invigorating to be involved in activities that really help others and a lot less invigorating to sit in the presence of God so He can work on us. If we neglect our alone time with God, our love for Christ can become polluted, not by sin, but by our love for doing, rather than being with Him. We are told to put Christ first and get to know Him through prayer, quiet time and the Word. Yet many of us rush through this time because we have so much to do for Him – we need to get about our Kingdom work. I think this limits our ministry effectiveness because God can't risk us infecting others with our polluted love for Him. How can we effectively spill out for others if we've neglected to be adequately filled by Him? Our work for Christ must flow out of our love for Him. Too often our work is fueled by feeling a sense of accomplishment, while in reality, we're running on empty because we forgot to fuel up. In Revelation 2:3-4 we are warned, *"You have persevered and have endured hardships for my name, and have not grown weary. Yet I hold this against you: you have forsaken your first love."*

Our work for Christ must flow out of our love for Him.

I have been around some people who appear almost saintly in their behavior toward someone in need, but once I've spent some time with them and watched their behavior, I start to question their motives for serving. In Hosea 7:8 it speaks of a flat cake that has not been turned over so it is only half-baked. Sometimes a person who appears to really want to help someone, is similar to a half-baked cake. Loving and compassionate on one-side, the other side has not been submitted to God, and has self-serving, secret agendas. Someone who is more focused on how they look to others than the person they are helping can do more harm than good. Sadly, the person being helped gets caught in the middle by this grandiose show of assistance that in reality, is a self-righteous act, less focused on the ongoing development of the person being served. But God sees and He cares. He sees the actions and the heart behind the actions. In Matthew 6:1-4 there is a lot of instruction in how we should help, *"Be careful not to do your 'acts of righteousness' before men, to be seen by them. If you do, you will have no reward from your Father in heaven. So when you give to the needy, do not*

announce it with trumpets, as the hypocrites do in the synagogues and on the streets, to be honored by men. I tell you the truth, they have received their reward in full. But when you give to the needy, do not let your left hand know what your right hand is doing, so that your giving may be in secret. Then your Father, who sees what is done in secret, will reward you." We must decide if we are going to chase success or significance, temporal or eternal work, public or private formation, approval by man or transformation by God. We must know what our end game is because it sets the rules for how we play.

If we want God to shape our world view and perspectives, things which shape our opinions, it is important to be with Him, not just do for Him. In Philippians 2:1-2 we are told, *If you have any encouragement from being united with Christ, if any comfort from His love, if an fellowship with the Spirit, if any tenderness and compassion, then make my joy complete by being like-minded, having the same love, being one in spirit and purpose.* If we are to become imitators of Christ we must grow in godly wisdom and knowledge. In Isaiah 45:19 God says, *"I have not spoken in secret, from somewhere in a land of darkness; I have not said to Jacob's descendants, 'Seek me in vain.' I, the Lord, speak the truth; I declare what is right."* Godly wisdom and knowledge are best found through the study of His Word, time spent in prayer and with mature Christians, but most importantly, solitary time with God. In Psalm 25:14 we are told, *The Lord confides in those who fear Him; He makes His covenant known to them.*

God wants us to know Him and we should continually be growing in our knowledge of Him, but I also know knowledge without action is wasted. If we don't do what we know we should do, it doesn't really matter that we know. David Roper says, "The main thing is not to know more things, but to live out the things we know." Our heart's desire should be to love the Lord our God with all our heart, soul and mind and to follow Him in grateful obedience. We do not need to know or understand the secrets of God. We just need to be with Him and do what He shows us to do.

Questions to Ponder:

1. Have you ever struggled with wanting to earn your relationship with God? Explain.
2. Reflect on the fact that God said He was pleased with Jesus before He began His ministry. What should that teach us about our God?
3. There is nothing mandated or forced about God's love. Can that be one of the reasons we may neglect our time with Him? Explain.
4. If the main thing is not to know more things, but to live out what we know, what do you need to start or stop doing?

Application

PREMISE NINE: What if God is more focused on developing my relationship with Him than on what I can do for Him?

IF THIS IS TRUE, then perhaps God wants us to engage more with, and do less for, those we help.

"We should not just provide resources for people.
We must also build resources within people."
– Lois Tupyi

Relationships Matter:

Similar to our *doing* for rather than *being with* God, we also like to *do* for people, not necessarily *be with* people, especially those we don't know, and the reasons are often the same. Doing is about accomplishment and it feels good and shows progress quickly. Being is about relationship, and relationships require time and an investment of ourselves. Relationships are also messy and can be uncomfortable at times. Who wouldn't prefer to just do, feeling a sense of accomplishment and then be done, rather than risk an ongoing relationship with someone where progress is hard to determine and finishing is obscure?

> A community built on ongoing dependence, rather than striving toward a healthy interdependency, is not healthy - it is enabling.

Sometimes our ministry or programs can become more important than the people we are offering them to. We become focused on success, disguising it under the cloak of compassion, but really only serve our own need or the needs of the ministry. We plan activities that don't draw people closer to Christ and while claiming to give God the glory, we make sure we're front and center when there's applause or accolades. If it's all exposed, we are more focused on ourselves, our agendas and organizations than our God. When ministry efforts become primarily focused on managing what has been built, we move from big 'K' Kingdom, which is the work of God's hands, to worshiping our little 'k' kingdoms, the works of our hands. If what we do doesn't make the person better long-term, what does it matter if it makes both them and us feel better for the moment?

Too often organizations and churches create programs that ultimately end up creating a community of people dependent on those who serve them. People return again and again to have their needs met and over time develop community with those who serve them. The problem is most relationships stay at the acquaintance level, not addressing the deeper, hidden needs that actually are the cause of the surface needs being addressed. These casual relationships seldom move beyond surface dialog, missing opportunities for deeper conversations focused on building long-term relationships that could promote transformation.

A community built on ongoing dependence, rather than striving toward a healthy interdependency, is not healthy - it is enabling. In Acts 4:32 we read, *All the believers were one in heart and mind. No one claimed that any of his possessions was his own, but they shared everything they had.* Everyone contributed to the good of the community. Would it not be a much better investment of both time and money if we focused on activities that promoted mutual contribution, developed through healthy relationships, where all parties involved shared common goals? In my opinion we should stop pursuing ministry efforts that enable people to feel better but do nothing to improve them or make their life better. Instead we should create opportunities for people to find community with others, not driven by their ongoing need, but rather an awareness that they too have something to offer to the community.

These types of helping communities are seldom developed and there are a lot of reasons why, but one of the main ones is people don't know how. How does one enter into a relationship with someone outside their social circle in ways that employ healthy boundaries, mutual engagement and common goals? Having entered into these types of relationships for over twenty years, I would have to say it must be done cautiously, with knowledge and great awareness of what one should and shouldn't do in the relationship – before it begins! I've seen so many well-meaning, compassionate people take someone into their heart or home to help them, only to have it become a nightmare they can't wake up from, because they don't know how to get out once it becomes unhealthy.

Philippians 4:8 gives us a solid foundation for right thinking, which will prompt right actions and help set a firm foundation on which to build a transformative relationship. *Finally, brothers, whatever is true, whatever is noble, whatever is right, whatever is pure, whatever is lovely, whatever is admirable – if anything is excellent or praiseworthy – think about such things*. What does it mean to be:

- **True –** Is it truth according to God's Word? This means we cannot just believe someone is telling the whole truth. We need to search for the true story behind any situation, which means time is spent hearing the story from different perspectives and then seeking God's truth for what the next steps are.

- **Noble –** Is it honorable, worthy of respect and of high integrity? This means we check our motives for why we want to enter into the relationship to begin with. A relationship motivated by our own need will seldom help address another person's real need.

- **Right –** Is it right and correct based on collective spiritual discernment? We must go to God's Word, our prayer closets and God's people to seek God's right for any relationship.

- **Pure –** Is it unpolluted by the world – holy? This again is checking motives of all parties involved and not letting the world's perspective or others push ideas and agendas that are not Gods. We need to purify our ideas and decisions with God before we make a decision to enter into a relationship.

- **Lovely –** Is it undefiled with godly characteristics? Will this relationship be pleasing to God or will we have to compromise our beliefs to enter into it? What is right is often compromised over what is convenient and a relationship entered into for the wrong reasons will never be right.

- **Admirable –** Will the end result be something to be held in high regard and emulated? Casual, uninvolved relationships that provide a roof over someone's head or other resources, without mentorship, will not have admirable endings.

- **Excellent or praise-worthy –** Will the relationship glorify God? To know Christ better and to represent Him well is a lofty goal for all of us to strive towards in the relationships we engage in.

I believe if these biblical virtues were used to filter how we respond to someone in need, it would change what we do, how we do it and why we do it. Let us seek relationships that move from being fear-driven to grace-released, from entitlement-justified to humility-empowered, from self-protective to selfless-giving because healthy relationships propagate healthy people.

Wired to Participate:

Doing something for someone doesn't build up anyone but the doer. In fact when we do things for someone without involving them, we further substantiate their false belief that we are superior and they are weak, we are blessed and they are needy, we can but they cannot, and so on and so on. Our actions limit positive enrichment when the only one involved is the helper and we are told in 1 Corinthians 10:24, *Nobody should seek his own good, but the good of others.* God delights in giving us good things. But He delights more in who we are as His children. He can withhold as easily as give, especially when the receiving becomes more important than the becoming. We should provide resources for people when God gives us the ability, but never at the expense of someone's personal growth. When our gifts become more important or interfere with helping someone grow into who God has given them capacity to be, our gifts become chains, rather than a road toward the freedom found in living the life God has designed.

Each person is a work of art, signed by God. His fingerprints are all over us. Part of this unique fingerprinting is the fact that God has hard-wired all of us to participate, to want to be engaged. In Ecclesiastes 3:13 we read, *That every man may eat and drink, and find satisfaction in all his toil* – this is the gift of God. My personal opinion is that much of the unrest, violence, high suicide rates, drug use and out-of-control anger exists because people are not actively engaged in positive ways within their own lives. Our current helping system is upside down. Factors that used to motivate people to provide and care for their immediate family members no longer exist. People are rewarded and receive more assistance if they do less, remain unmarried and have children because aid is based on the number of dependents in the home. Sadly, many children don't have a father figure in their home, much less in their life. The single mother is usually at her wits end trying to make it all work. Needless to say all of this free help provides barely enough assistance to survive, yet they do survive and ultimately become trapped in lifestyles beneath their capabilities. Millions of people have fallen victim and dependent on this ongoing help, unable and often unwilling, to do the hard work to rise above it. Not only is participation not required, it is unlawful to ask people to do something to receive federal aid. In today's society the less you do, the more you receive and the less is expected of you.

People with initiative and drive who want to take proactive steps to improve their lives have difficulty transitioning out of dependency to self-sufficiency. They may feel penalized initially as resources are removed immediately as their income increases. I'm unaware of any programs that wean people off assistance slowly, which would give them time to find affordable, new resources to replace the free resources they have lost. In my experience, as they try to get their footing in this new lifestyle they are pursuing, few survive the climb out. Without others in their lives who believe in them, to help them navigate new methods of living, most will quit trying and give up, resigning themselves to a life of dependency and mediocracy. The unfairness of it just breaks my heart and I imagine, God's too. In Isaiah 5:20 we are warned, *Woe to those who call evil good and good evil, who put darkness for light and light for darkness, who put bitter for sweet and sweet for bitter.* I believe this twisted, confining way of assistance will not go unnoticed by God.

In my opinion, initiative, drive and desire have been stolen, replaced with apathy, hopelessness and entitlement. As a result, the children who grow up in these homes dependent upon assistance will seldom witness the adults who care for them pursuing avenues to improve their lives or livelihoods. This is why I'm so passionate about offering compassion that has redemptive power. We cannot afford to be complacent, apathetic or uninvolved. We need to give people a chance to get back into the game of life and *"Speak up for those who cannot speak for themselves, for the rights of all who are destitute. Speak up and judge fairly; defend the rights of the poor and needy."* Proverbs 31:8-9. This is best done by engaging in relationships that promote personal involvement, reveal undiscovered potential and believe God's hand and His plan is on every life on this earth. To do any less is just not our best.

All of us like the feeling of accomplishment we get when we do something productive. This is exactly why it is so important to engage those we help. They too need to feel valued and important, a contributor, rather than set to the side as if they are too broken to be part of the solution. In Proverbs 22:6 we are told, *Train a child in the way he should go, and when he is old he will not turn from it.* What if this applies to all God's children, child and adult? Could it be that Solomon is talking about how we should help people identify the unique ways God has gifted them? How exciting would it be to help people understand, almost treasure hunt, for their natural abilities and how God has personally crafted them? I think if this was done more often it would help people move into the abundant life God has for us. Most people who need assistance are asked about their need. Focus is on what they don't have, what they can't do and what they need someone else to do for them. If we can learn to engage others in their own solutions by focusing on what they can do, what they already have and honing their skills, it would be a win-win for everyone involved. So much of the time people in need only think of what they lack or their weaknesses. Through relationships, we can create opportunities to speak life-defining words to others, helping them find their true identity in Christ. Mark Batterson says, "The right word spoken at the right time can make an eternal difference." We should help identify individuals' strengths and talents so they can use these gifts to better themselves, their lives and the lives of those they are responsible for.

Transformative Love:

God's love is transformative. If His love was just a feel good, I'd-give-you-the-world type of love, He would give us everything we wanted because the world is literally at His fingertips, in fact, formed by His fingertips. Yet God seems to want more for us. He wants to transform us into who He created us to be, moving us into the wholeness of life He has given us the potential to live. Love that doesn't focus on the person, but is driven by performance, might be called love, but is it? Would it be better to call it pity or sympathy or empathy, but not love? In 1 Corinthians 13:4-7 we are told, *Love is patient, love is kind. It does not envy, it does not boast, it is not proud. It is not rude, it is not self-seeking, it is not easily angered, it keeps no record of wrongs. Love does not delight in evil but rejoices with the truth. It always protects, always trusts, always hopes, always perseveres.* This kind of love calls us to put ourselves and our agendas aside and enter into a relational love that is transforming, not just performing. This love is focused on building others up more than looking successful. We are told in Ephesians 4:29, *Do not let any unwholesome talk come out of your mouths, but only what is helpful for building others up according to their needs, that it may benefit those who listen.* If we want to model God's love, we cannot just focus on giving people what they think they need or want. We must be willing to enter into relationships that have the potential to help them become all they can be, to learn behaviors that can enrich and improve lives and families' futures. If God wants more for us than making us feel good with the stuff of life – should we not also want more for those we help?

Transformative love begins on the inside of the person and works its way out into the public eye. Anytime we try to fix the outside without first working on the inside we ultimately fail. Changing a habit does not mean it changes the heart. God is always examining the heart and tracking progress by it. We want to see progress and often look for change before it is even developed enough to be revealed. Initially, only God sees what is happening in the heart and for many of us, that's not good enough. We need to see before we can believe there is fruit from our efforts. Yet in Hebrews 11:1 we are told, *Now faith is being sure of what we hope for and certain of what we do not see.* Do we have the faith to do our part and trust God is working on the heart?

I think it's human nature to want to see success from our efforts. Why would we pursue something that seems to be failing or seems to have failed? What could possibly be our motivation to stay the course and persevere? Early in my ministry I had pastors asking for statistics on how many of those we served began attending their churches. I was unsure how to answer, because truth be known, we didn't know. We were planting seeds, tending new growth and encouraging people to plug into a church, but having good numbers to quantify our work was hard to come by. As I spent time in prayer I felt God share that if getting to see the harvest, in other words, picking the fruit that matured, was what was needed to persevere, then our services would be limited. I became convinced that to be His Kingdom worker, we need to do the work, without the need to know the results. In reality, we don't even know what it is God is trying to grow so how can we know if it's successful? We only know what we think people need, which is often what they've asked for, but God knows what transformative work He's doing in and through them. Sometimes what may look like a failure to us, could be the win He's been waiting for: perhaps a heart softened, a disruptive spirit starting to break or some small opening starting to let Him in. In Romans 8:20-21 we read, *For the creation was subjected to frustration, not by its own choice, but by the will of the one who subjected it, in hope that the creation itself will be liberated from its bondage to decay and brought into the glorious freedom of the children of God.* God has transformation on His mind and He subjects us to whatever is needed to liberate each of us from death to freedom. God needs Kingdom workers willing to play whatever small part He gives them in His life-changing, life-claiming work of transformation, who are willing to leave the results to Him. He can only use us in His grand plan when we don't care what part we play and we don't push to know results.

Struggling through these quantifying questions was when I first realized we cannot successfully count transformation. How do you know when hope is birthed, when a sin is confessed in the soul, when a heart opens to God? We don't know, so we can't count it. That is why I've come to think of it as the *immeasurably more* mentioned in Ephesians 3:20-21, *Now to Him who is able to do immeasurably more than all we ask or imagine, according to His power that is at work within us, to Him be glory in the church and in Christ Jesus throughout all generations, for ever and ever! Amen.* Transformative work is all about the heart changes and things we cannot easily see to count or measure – it's more, so much more. Every time transformation happens, it's a life changed by the touch of our Heavenly Father's hand that not only changes their life, but the lives of those who come after them. Let's choose to live out the words in Colossians 3:23-24, *Whatever you do, work at it with all your heart, as working for the Lord, not for men, since you know that you will receive an inheritance from the Lord as a reward. It is the Lord Christ you are serving.* One day, on the other side of heaven, we will get to see the *"immeasurably more"* that was a result in what seemed like some small and seemingly insignificant role God allowed us to play in His transformative work.

Clinging Too Tightly:

It's common to want more for the person we help than they do. They may want our stuff, money or other material and physical help, but they don't want to do the hard work of improving their life –often because they don't believe they have the ability to change even if they wanted to. Doing anything *for* someone, rather than *with* someone, weakens, not strengthens, in the long run. When someone is not ready for redemptive, restorative compassion, we have to learn to let them go. Too often we try to please, compromise or entice, trying to keep them interested in what we know they need. The reality is, most of us have to reach the end of ourselves before we are open to real help from someone else.

...most of us have to reach the end of ourselves before we are open to real help from someone else.

I have found it is important to not engage in meaningless debates with people who do not want to learn, but only want to argue. We waste valuable time trying to convince people who do not want to listen to what we're saying, and at some point it becomes two opposing sides trying to win the argument. I think we need to learn how to let go and trust God when people aren't ready for what we offer. I have found there are always others who want to be helped in meaningful ways and we should shift our attention to them. Jesus didn't waste energy trying to convince anyone of His cause. And He instructed His disciples in Matthew 10:14, *"If anyone will not welcome you or listen to your words, shake the dust off your feet when you leave that home or town."* We can waste precious time and energy trying to convince others of things they either have no interest in or disagree with. Let us look for God's open doors and not stand knocking at doors that are tightly closed to us.

The Prodigal Son story is a good example of letting go and trusting God. Let's pick it up in Luke 15:11-13 ...*"There was a man who had two sons. The younger one said to his father, 'Father, give me my share of the estate.'*

So he divided his property between them. Not long after that, the younger son got together all he had, set off for a distant country and there squandered his wealth in wild living." When I read between the lines, I believe the father knew his son would leave and squander his inheritance, making foolish choices and engaging in destructive lifestyles. But the story doesn't tell us the father tried to convince him to stay by compromising, bargaining or enticing him with promises of things his son might have found attractive. The father let him go, despite the difficult days that were ahead, continuing to love and look for his return – but he still let him go. If we were to hear the rest of the story, I imagine this son was ready to live life differently when he returned. Humbled and changed, he was probably ready to become responsible and do the hard work of living a full and productive life. Because his son was now ready, the father could invest in his son and their future.

God does the same thing with us. He'll let us go and leave us alone to wallow in whatever lifestyles and choices we want to make. But He never quits looking for us, anticipating our return and when we're ready He's willing and ready to invest time in us. I'm sure there is a heavenly celebration when we return and then God goes to work, refining, reshaping and restoring us into who He created us to be. Often the lesson can't be learned without the wayward journey being allowed. When we don't allow someone to make their own choices, even when we know the way will be harmful, we potentially interfere in what God can and will do in and through them once they've reached the end of themselves. We can't do what someone needs to do for themselves and when we try, we will usually fail and they will certainly not learn. Life lessons are usually learned in the doing, seldom in the classroom. We gain experience by living through our poor choices and good choices then become the fruit of those experiences. Let us learn how to let go when we've done all we can, trusting them to God and hoping one day they'll return to us, ready to engage and make a change in their life.

Questions to Ponder:

1. Do you agree that *doing for* others is easier than *being in* a relationship with them? Explain.

2. List your own thoughts about my comment that a lot of what is happening in our nation is because people are not engaged in their own lives.

3. Do you agree we can change a habit, but God must transform the heart for lasting transformation? Explain.

4. If the *immeasurably more* is about transformative works that are difficult to quantify, but life-changing, how do we statistically track progress?

⁕ Premise TEN

"Time is short, none of us knows how long we have.
Live each day as if it were your last – for some day it will be."

–Billy Graham

What if God gives me, not what I deserve or have earned, but rather what I need to mature in my faith?

Entitled:

I hesitate to even write this part of my story because I'm not proud of it, but it was something God needed me to recognize and understand about myself. As I've mentioned before, from my earliest memories I feel I have had a relationship with God. That said, my journey has taken detours down dark alleys where I hoped God would follow me since I was not following Him. For the most part though, I have tried to live a good life, love God and my fellowman and do the right thing. At the time of this recovery I had been in ministry activities for nineteen years, committed to understanding God's Kingdom call and executing it to the best of my ability. When the recovery wasn't going according to my plan and other health issues, totally unrelated to this surgery, also seemed to be going wrong, I was confused. After all, I had spent my days and a good portion of my evenings doing His work. I had worked hard at overcoming sin's patterns which had entrapped me in the past and I loved God with all my heart. I just couldn't understand why I wasn't being healed.

Then it hit me like a ton of bricks – I subconsciously felt that as a Christ-follower, I had earned the right to be healed. When I realized what was at the core of my discouragement and confusion, I felt sick to my stomach. God didn't and doesn't owe me anything! I'm a sinner, fickle in nature, divided in heart and just plain not good enough to deserve the gift of grace already available to me through the death of His Son Jesus Christ. Thank goodness He hasn't given me what I deserve, what I really am entitled to! Thank God for the gift of grace and the promise of eternal salvation, in spite of what I deserve. God had to reveal this to me if I was going to mature in my faith.

There you have it. It isn't pretty and it's hard to confess, but I don't think I'm the only Christ-follower who might have some entitlement issues. For those who are able to relate, confess with me to our Heavenly Father and let us claim this promise found in Psalm 103: 12 *As far as the east is from the west, so far has He removed our transgressions from us.* Thank the Lord He does not give us what we deserve - He gives us so much more!

Feeling entitled is a heart matter and is actually what caused Joseph's problems from the beginning. His brothers were jealous and felt entitled to the favor Joseph seemed to be receiving. At the end of this story, we see Joseph test them to determine their hearts. Had they changed or were they still trying to usurp and take undeserved power? In Genesis chapter 44:33 we see Judah, one of the brothers say, *"Now then, please let your servant remain here as my lord's slave in place of the boy, and let the boy return with his brothers."* It appeared to Joseph they were sorry and humble, no longer acting entitled, but displayed a brokenness as they struggled with what they had done years ago to their brother Joseph. Then we read the best part of the story in Genesis 45:4-5, *Then Joseph said to his brothers, "Come close to me." When they had done so, he said, "I am your brother Joseph, the one you sold into Egypt! And now, do not be distressed and do not be angry with yourselves for selling me here, because it was to save lives that God sent me ahead of you."* The brothers were not going to receive what they deserved, but rather Joseph extended undeserved grace. Only God can make a promise and then work it out to produce His miracle years later. Only God is entitled, worthy and deserves our utter and complete devotion.

Entitlement:

Many people, including Christians, suffer from an attitude of entitlement, believing good behavior should produce positive benefits. But God has not promised an easy or fair life, just a fulfilled life. When we feel entitled, it blocks selfless love and causes division in community. When we feel entitled, we become self-focused, not on what is best for all, but what is best for me. Entitlement buys into the lie that because we think we deserve it, we are entitled to it. Christian entitlement results from falsely believing that if we try hard, do good works and love God then He owes us – our life should be protected from harm, we should reap benefits from our labor and the blessing of the Lord should be obvious.

> But God has not promised an easy or fair life, just a fulfilled life.

I think this often happens because we want to use God more than honor Him. We try as hard as we can to be a good Christian and think we should reap a reward for our good behavior. We can even walk with a false sense of security that things won't go as wrong if we're doing everything we can to live right. Perhaps, in our own selfish way, we secretly believe God will bless us because as His child we are entitled to a better, easier life than someone who doesn't acknowledge Him. This is not true because there are no guaranteed outcomes from worshiping God. If we're not careful this type of attitude can make a mockery of why we love God - not to know Him or become like Him, but to ease our earthly journey and enjoy the blessings we believe we deserve. When we seek after God for our own rewards, rather than trying to die to self, we do not glorify God but rather expect Him to treat us favorably. This entitlement attitude soon undermines any submissive spirit God may be trying to grow in our soul and soon our Christian walk becomes more about using God than allowing Him to use us.

An attitude of entitlement, with preset expectations and conditions, limits God's ability to use us in Kingdom work. When things don't work out and blessings don't come despite our best efforts, these unmet expectations can cause us to doubt, become discouraged and give up. Sometimes we even move out of Kingdom work, questioning the validity of God or our call because we felt entitled to success and when it doesn't come, we quit. We become convinced that what we're doing must not be from God because it isn't working out like we expected. I believe there are times when this lack of worldly success is exactly what God has in mind. He is using it to help us learn, reposition or even redirect our efforts. Maturing in God's love means we can accept His love without putting requirements on it.

God's Kingdom is not about earning and deserving. It is about believing and receiving, which means we move away from what we think we deserve and accept what we get as God given. Too many of us have bought into the ideology that if we live well, life will go well. If we believe this, it can quickly develop into a works-based attitude, based on what we do and how we do it. Part of the danger in a works-based theology is that when it doesn't go well, we blame ourselves, others or God. Romans 3:23-24 tells us, *For all have sinned and fall short of the glory of God, and are justified freely by His grace through the redemption that came by Christ Jesus.* We cannot let our failures, short comings or imperfections separate us from God. In a works-based theology, when we behave inappropriately, we become fearful we might get what we deserve. It's at those times we must remember God offers unconditional love and undeserved grace. He doesn't bless us when we behave well or punish us when we let ourselves or others down. Yet it is important to understand actions rise from within our heart and inappropriate behaviors and attitudes indicate heart issues. In Joel 2:13 we are told, *Rend your heart and not your garments. Return to the Lord your God, for He is gracious and compassionate, slow to anger and abounding in love, and He relents from sending calamity.* It has never been about *what we do* but has always been about *whose we are.* Rather than demanding what we feel entitled to or hiding in fear because we've failed, let us cry out to God and stand in His strength, claiming victory in whatever situation life brings us. *Then they cried out to the Lord in their trouble, and He delivered them from their distress.* Psalm 107:6.

Do All Things Well:

We are a culture that despises the small things. Focus is on being great, doing great and possessing great things. To strive for greatness is inbred in us and Zechariah 4:10 asks, *"Who despises the day of small things?..."* I think many do, yet in God's world size doesn't seem to matter and substance seems to be everything. God often uses unknown people, doing seemingly insignificant, small tasks to accomplish historic, amazing things. If we want to see a miracle or be a miracle, we cannot wait for the one big thing, the one big moment that will put us before the large audience. God calls us to be faithful in the small things He brings our way because the significance of something is usually seen in the rearview mirror. Most of the time we don't know what God is doing until we look back. We don't have to influence millions, we just need to let God use us to influence one, who may influence millions. Vaclav Havel said, "The real test of a man is not when he plays the role that he wants for himself, but when he plays the role destiny has for him."

I think a great biblical example of how a small thing can have great significance is found in the story of the donkey owners in Luke 19:29-34, *As [Jesus] approached Bethphage and Bethany at the hill called the Mount of Olives, He sent two of His disciples, saying to them, "Go to the village ahead of you, and as you enter it, you will find a colt tied there, which no one has ever ridden. Untie it and bring it here. If anyone asks you, 'Why are you untying it?' tell him, 'The Lord needs it.'" Those who were sent went and found it just as He had told them. As they were untying the colt, its owners asked them, "Why are you untying the colt?" They replied, "The Lord needs it."* Jesus' triumphant entry on the donkey is embedded in history, representing humility and obedience to His Father. The crowds wanted Him to enter with force, perhaps on a stallion representing power and prestige. Jesus chose the donkey to show His submission to God, and to make the point that He was under a different authority – God. The donkey's owners played a small, but significant role in this event without understanding the bigger picture. They gave up something they legally owned, and through obedience in a small thing, provided a much-needed prop in a historical event. Let us pray to sense the small things God puts on our hearts that might play an important part in His plan, no matter how seemingly insignificant they seem and even if we don't get to see the final outcome.

If we want to be involved in significant work, do all things as if they have great significance.

Sometimes an entitlement attitude can affect how we view worth and we find ourselves subconsciously thinking some things are beneath us. We all like to do tasks that seem important or are admired, but I have found it's the seemingly insignificant things that often determine success or failure. God will never give us the big things to do if we are too important to do the little things well. Luke 16:10-11 instructs us, *"Whoever can be trusted with very little can also be trusted with much, and whoever is dishonest with very little will also be dishonest with much. So if you have not been trustworthy in handling worldly wealth, who will trust you with true riches?"* God doesn't bless negligence and requires us to do Kingdom work with diligence. He wants us to do our part as well as we can with what we've been given. I think it is easy to be "all in" when we're asked to be part of something significant. Can we also be eagerly "all in" when the task or role seems small, irrelevant and perhaps even insignificant? Oswald Chambers said, "All God's revelations are sealed until they are opened to us by obedience...Obey God in the thing He shows you and instantly the next thing is opened up...God will never reveal more truth about Himself until you have obeyed what you know already." If we want to be involved in significant work, do all things as if they have great significance.

When we help people through our programs, I can almost always predict the success they will have by how well they do the things asked of them initially that don't seem that important. I have found that if they cannot or will not do these initial things well, they will struggle advancing to the more significant things later. We can't grant more responsibility until they have a proven record, through behavior, with the small things. I think God also wants us to prove ourselves by doing the lesser things well before He advances us into deeper Kingdom work. The servant with the single talent failed because he didn't think it had enough value to invest time and money in. In Matthew 25:28-29 we see his reward stripped away, *"'Take the talent from him and give it to the one who has the ten talents. For everyone who has will be given more, and he will have an abundance. Whoever does not have, even what he has will be taken from him.'"* In contrast, in Matthew 25:21 we read what the Master said to the one given the ten talents, *"...'Well done, good and faithful servant! You have been faithful with a few things; I will put you in charge of many things. Come and share your master's happiness!'"* God does not give us what we think we deserve, but rather what He knows we need to mature in our faith. Mark Batterson summarizes it well, "In God's book, success is spelled stewardship. It's making the most of the time, talent and treasure God has given you. It's doing the best you can with what you have where you are." God needs to finish His work in us before He can advance greater Kingdom work through us.

Finish Well:

We must learn to live in the power of His first coming with the hope found in the promise of His second one. Hebrews 3:14 reminds us, *We have come to share in Christ if we hold firmly till the end the confidence we had at first.* For me, it seems I am in a constant battle between two worlds. I can feel entitled, then surrendered; frustrated, then content; fearful, then at rest; irritated, then patient; restless, then peace-filled; engaged in Kingdom work, then fighting a personal battle. Oh to grow my faith so I will not just start well, but push through to finish well. My personal belief is that finishing well requires ongoing growth and continual maturing in our faith. Kingdom work is soul work which means it is eternal work – it passes through to eternity when we pass on. The things we do with our hands are temporary and may be important, but not as important as the lasting changes that are made in our soul as we strive to mature.

There are many Scriptures dedicated to finishing well. Philippians 3:12-14 states, *Not that I have already obtained all this, or have already been made perfect, but I press on to take hold of that for which Christ Jesus took hold of me...Forgetting what is behind and straining toward what is ahead, I press on toward the goal to win the prize for which God has called me heavenward in Christ Jesus.* I have always found it easier to start than push through the mundane to the end. Compassion that has redemptive power will always require us to commit to the long haul, which is one of the reasons it is so seldom done. Charity can be done quickly, easily and without much effort, but entering into a relationship to help others mature in Christ – requires a commitment. Let us draw encouragement from these words in Hebrews 10:35-36, *So do not throw away your confidence; it will be richly rewarded. You need to persevere so that when you have done the will of God, you will receive what He has promised.*

Doing the right thing will not always produce the results we want or expect and can complicate our ability to finish well. It requires us to move from basing success or failure on the outcome of our efforts, and base it on the obedience of our heart. If we do not learn this lesson ourselves we will struggle teaching it to others attempting to improve their own lives. This is especially true during times when no one can see progress. Giving up midstream can result in giving up on ourselves or God. Someone trying to improve their life can get discouraged and want to quit because it gets hard along the way, but the hard times are when we learn the most. I read these five steps Charles Stanley had written in a devotional and added some of my thoughts because I think they apply to persevering well:

- "First, recall past victories, recounting times when God has been faithful in the past to give encouragement for the present." As Winston Churchill said, "Remembering what He has done gives us courage for what He will do." To persevere well we must draw strength from the past as we lean in and embrace our future.

- "Second, examine your motivation. What is really driving you in this trial, your personal goals or your devotion to God?" Sometimes when we are wearing out it is because we want out. Doing things without God's strength can feel burdensome and unrewarding. In Matthew 11:28-30 we are told, *"Come to me all you who are weary and burdened, and I will give you rest. Take my yoke upon you and learn from me, for I am gentle and humble in heart, and you will find rest for your souls. For my yoke is easy and my burden is light."*

- "Third, reject discouragement. Well-meaning people can sometimes quench your faith. Listen to and obey the Father, who will never fail nor forsake you." It is easy for others to offer well-intended, but misguided advice, when they do not know the past and do not understand the goal. Winston Churchill said, "Success is not final, failure is not fatal. It is the courage to continue that counts."

- "Fourth, recognize the real purpose for the battle. Nothing touches your life unless it first passes through the Lord's protective hand." This means there's a benefit for you in this challenge if you'll persevere through to the end. Mark Batterson reminds us, "It's not my job to tell God how to do His job. I simply need to get into God's presence and see what God does."

- "Fifth, rely upon God's power for victory. Trust the Lord so much that the victory already is decided in your mind." Trust God and trust His methods. Warren Wiersbe reminds us, "There is a difference between 'fruit' and 'results'. Results are counted and soon become silent statistics, but living fruit remains and continues to multiply to the glory of God."

If the Lord should return today, what will He find us doing? Will we be busy about His work or be found enjoying the comforts of His blessings to the neglect of the call He placed on us? Oswald Chambers said, "May God save us from Christian service which is nothing more than the reaction of a disappointed, crushed heart, seeking relief from sorrow through social service. Christian service is the vital, unconscious result of the life of a believer in Jesus." In John 17:15-18 we see Jesus pray for you and me to be about His work, *"My prayer is not that you take them out of the world but that you protect them from the evil one. They are not of the world, even as I am not of it. Sanctify them by the truth; your word is truth. As you sent me into the world, I have sent them into the world."* Let us persevere to the end and not grow weary or complacent so we can live out the words in Colossians 4:17, ...*"See to it that you complete the work you have received in the Lord."*

Questions to Ponder:

1. Do you agree Christ-followers can develop an attitude of entitlement? Explain.

2. If God's Kingdom is not about earning and deserving but believing and receiving, how well do you live this out in your own life? Explain.

3. Do you agree that we should do all things as if they have great significance because we don't really understand the significance of most things until we look back? Explain.

4. Is there something you started, motivated by God, but have not completed? Explain what and why not.

APPLICATION

PREMISE TEN: What if God gives me, not what I deserve or have earned, but rather what I need to mature in my faith?

IF THIS IS TRUE, we should strive to help others develop their full potential in Christ.

"It's possible to be in ministry and use people to get what we want instead of helping people to get what they need."

–Warren Wiersbe

Unsolicited Help:

At the writing of this book, our nation has been coping with the COVID-19 pandemic. This experience has been challenging, but also very revealing to me. Early in the crisis, food shelves became empty and everyone scrambled to feed and care for the children. The government feverishly worked on legislation to put money in our pockets, help businesses and those whose employment had been disrupted. What intrigued and dismayed me at the same time was related to something I had struggled with for a while but this crisis seemed to put my concern on steroids. In our community, but I imagine across the nation, there was an overwhelming response to help others, both individually and corporately. But this offered help did not engage or involve those being helped by asking if they wanted or even needed help. It appeared the assumption was made that people would not be able to care for themselves or their families and others must step in and do it for them. Since we assumed people needed help without asking or involving them, my personal fear was it would solidify this idea that people can't care for themselves and others must meet their needs – an assumption that is not necessarily correct and weakens families and our nation overall.

As the months have passed, helping efforts have not diminished, but rather grown and adapted to fulfill this narrative that we must feed the children. At first, in our community, food was offered for those who wanted to pick it up. Because the response was low, it was decided to start taking the food to people, using bus routes to determine drop off points. Over time, due to the large surpluses of food, the outreach was widened to include anyone wanting to be part of these food drops, regardless of need, only asking for the zip code of the recipients for statistical purposes. Other agencies and organizations have also stepped in to cover the weekends – everyone focused on making sure no one would go hungry, with few trying to discern if people truly were hungry.

I'm not advocating we shouldn't help meet food insecurity or any other real needs. To the contrary, I've dedicated a large part of my life to assisting those in need. What I am concerned about is that this precedent will become the standard for future crises. In my opinion it has not served to strengthen those struggling and will be hard to maintain for extended periods of time by those who are giving. I'm also concerned that those who received assistance have been removed from the responsibility of caring for their own families. I can't help but think this lack of involvement may affect their sense of worth, value, responsibility and now growing feelings of entitlement. Perpetuating this sort of mindset does not strengthen individuals, nor provide good role models for the children within the homes, who more than likely will expect similar help when they face a crisis as an adult. I believe, out of love and care for others, when we assist we should make sure we allow people opportunities to be strengthened, not weakened, walking with them during a challenging time, without usurping their personal responsibility for it. Warren Wiersbe said, "The best thing we can do for people is not to solve their problems for them, but so relate them to God's grace, that they will be enabled to solve their problems and not repeat them."

At one time, the two most motivating factors for people to work were to provide and care for their families and to improve life for themselves and those they cared for. These motivations no longer exist. People don't have to work to receive enough daily sustenance to survive and many adults don't believe they can change their future or their children's future. Most people living in chronic low-income or poverty situations do not know how to escape the lifestyle of need they've learned to navigate for survival. In my opinion this status quo of providing resources *for* people without building resources *within* people needs to change. People are not encouraged to develop their full potential when we do for them what they could learn and should do for themselves!

Senseless Shepherds:

It would be wonderful, but incorrect, to assume that everyone who provides assistance has pure motives. Throughout history, usurping power by keeping people dissatisfied, dependant and weak has proven effective in controlling and advancing agendas that are not beneficial to mankind. We read a warning in Isaiah 10:1-2, *Woe to those who make unjust laws, to those who issue oppressive decrees, to deprive the poor of their rights and rob my oppressed people of justice....* Dictators control people by keeping them weak, thinking for them and making them dependent on others for their daily sustenance. They tear down by lifting themselves up, take power by force and pervert truth rather than promote justice. Perverted authority happens when those in leadership positions use their money and power to control the very ones they are supposedly tasked to care for.

God has a severe warning found in Ezekiel 34:2-4 for those abusing their leadership status, *"...'This is what the Sovereign Lord says: Woe to the shepherds of Israel who only take care of themselves! Should not shepherds take care of the flock? You eat the curds, clothe yourselves with the wool and slaughter the choice animals, but you do not take care of the flock. You have not strengthened the weak or healed the sick or bound up the injured. You have not brought back the strays or searched for the lost. You have ruled them harshly and brutally.'"* Offering aid puts us, to some degree, in a place of power. We have something others need and our response determines if it will be self-defeating or uplifting to those receiving help.

Perverted authority happens when those in leadership positions use their money and power to control the very ones they are supposedly tasked to care for.

Sometimes those in leadership are just wicked but other times they are clueless, which Jeremiah 10:21 explains, *The shepherds are senseless and do not inquire of the Lord; so they do not prosper and all their flock is scattered.* I think it's hard to be a godly leader when I'm also a sin-filled person because of my inherent nature. Without God to guide and lead me, I can quickly lead others astray or provide help in a way that is self-elevating. Leaders cannot afford to build up themselves or their programs at the expense of those they serve. Whether it is done consciously or unconsciously, the result is still the same - we have not strengthened, but rather weakened, those God entrusted to our care.

Do we desire to see godly wisdom develop in others as much as we desire for it to come through us? In John 3:30, we see John understand his role clearly, *"He must become greater; I must become less."* As John Wesley said, "Let us know how to sit as well as to rise." I have to confess that I like being thought of as wise. I like feeling important. I like being perceived as one who hears from the Lord. I like opportunities to serve, teach and help others. What I should strive for is to share what God has given me in ways that raise up those I serve, elevating and helping them mature and move into the full potential God has given them. If our acts of compassion are void of redemptive power, they are confining not refining, restricting not uplifting and imprisoning not freeing. Isaiah 30:1,5 gives us a warning we should heed, *"Woe to the obstinate children," declares the Lord, "to those who carry out plans that are not mine, forming an alliance, but not by my Spirit, heaping sin upon sin; everyone will be put to shame because of a people useless to them, who bring neither help nor advantage, but only shame and disgrace."*

I can't close this section without a brief note on being unequally yoked. Many organizations recognize the advantage of partnering with churches because churches normally have a large volunteer base and programs that allow them to easily collect and distribute large quantities of resources. These partnerships are a win-win scenario for helping entities outside the church. Many churches also like to work with the community through partnerships that present opportunities the church may not otherwise be invited to participate in. All that said, when the church forms an alliance with anyone who stands between them and the person receiving help, the church loses its ability to begin a relationship and speak of the hope found in Christ. When we allow this to happen, the church loses its unique mission and becomes like the other secular organizations around it. Matthew 5:13 speaks of this, *"You are the salt of the earth. But if the salt loses its saltiness, how can it be made salty again? It is no longer good for anything, except to be thrown out and trampled by men…."* As Christians, our motivation and goals should be different than secular organizations because God has called us to be different. Let us not yoke together with anyone who will not allow us to speak of the hope found in Jesus Christ or enter into relationship with those we serve.

In our Corner:

I love the word picture found in Romans 8:34, *Who is He that condemns? Christ Jesus, who died – more than that, who was raised to life – is at the right hand of God and is also interceding for us.* Just picture it – God and Jesus are in our corner. With coaches like that how can we fail if we will just listen and follow Their plan? Abraham Lincoln said, "My concern is not whether God is on our side, but whether we are on His side." God and Jesus are in our corner and have our backs, we just need to make sure we go to Their corner to be refreshed, receive guidance and get pumped up to get back in the ring after we've been knocked around in life.

As I write this, I find myself reflecting on those who are in my corner and how important they are to me. Without their encouragement, instruction, correction and persevering through with me – even from the sideline – I would be unable to continue as I seek to live out my call to God's glory. My heart is sad that too many people feel alone, believing they don't have anyone in their corner fighting for and with them. I think everyone needs to know someone is on their team and believes in them and their potential, especially when they've taken so many blows they're struggling to stand. There are times when we all need to be reminded Jesus and God are working together with our best interest in mind. We all need someone willing to stay in the fight with us when others retreat. Someone who reminds us of who and whose we are when circumstances dictate we're less. Someone willing to push us back out or move us forward when we want to quit, run or under-perform. Someone who keeps the faith when doubt threatens to crack the foundation of our own faith. Someone willing to hold us up when weariness tries to take us down. This is what compassion with redemptive power is all about. Being willing to get in someone's corner and tell them they're not alone. God and Jesus sit together with watchful eyes and send others to stand and fight with each of us in the game of life. Are you ready and equipped for God to send you into someone's corner?

Spirit of God:

You have just invested time reading this book, but there is something pressing on me that I need to say – you can't do this redemptive compassion thing – not on your own. Redemptive Compassion requires the Holy Spirit to work within our spirits to accomplish things we cannot do on our own. Matthew 19:26 says, …*"With man this is impossible, but with God all things are possible."* We cannot transform someone – only God can. We can't create redemptive power – only God can. We can't save anyone from a life of need – only God can. We are insufficient to offer compassion that has redemptive power without involving God. But the good news is God has chosen us to partner with Him, to bring wholeness of life to others who find themselves in a struggle. To do this we must first understand we cannot do Kingdom work, holy work, without God's transforming power through His Spirit living within us. Isaiah 11:2-4 gives us insight into how the Spirit works, *The Spirit of the Lord will rest on him – the Spirit of wisdom and of understanding, the Spirit of counsel and of power, the Spirit of knowledge and of the fear of the Lord – and he will delight in the fear of the Lord. He will not judge by what he sees with his eyes, or decide by what he hears with his ears; but with righteousness he will judge the needy, with justice he will give decisions for the poor of the earth. He will strike the earth with the rod of his mouth; with the breath of his lips he will slay the wicked.* What hope those Scriptures should give us as we seek to love as God loves us!

But the good news is God has chosen us to partner with Him.

When the Spirit is at work within us, we will see the fruit of that Spirit as listed In Galatians 5:22-25, *But the fruit of the Spirit is love, joy, peace, patience, kindness, goodness, faithfulness, gentleness and self-control. Against such things there is no law. Those who belong to Christ Jesus have crucified the sinful nature with its passions and desires. Since we live by the Spirit, let us keep in step with the Spirit.* When the Spirit of God lives within us, He does the internal work we need done, equipping us to participate in the external work of offering compassion with redemptive power to others.

Compassion that has redemptive power is not a quick fix. There's no quick answer to the transformative power God can work through us, to work within another, except through relationships. We see how Jesus selected and then lived with and taught the twelve disciples He mentored the last three years of His life. Even with this close relationship, the disciples did not understand most of what Jesus said and did until after His death when He gave them the Holy Spirit. They had only been given a glimpse of heaven while He was on earth. 1 Corinthians 13:12 says, *Now we see but a poor reflection; then we shall see face to face. Now I know in part; then I shall know fully, even as I am fully known.* It was after Jesus' resurrection, while speaking to His disciples that He gave them further instruction in Luke 24:49, *"...I am going to send you what my Father has promised; but stay in the city until you have been clothed with power from on high."* Offering compassion with redemptive power requires the Holy Spirit. God has said in Zechariah 4:6, *"...'Not by might, nor by power, but by my Spirit.'..."* 1 Corinthians 2:9-13 clarifies for us, *However, as it is written: "No eye has seen, no ear has heard, no mind has conceived what God has prepared for those who love him" – but God has revealed it to us by His Spirit. The Spirit searches all things, even the deep things of God. For who among men knows the thoughts of a man except the man's spirit within him? In the same way no one knows the thoughts of God except the Spirit of God. We have not received the spirit of the world but the Spirit who is from God, that we may understand what God has freely given us. This is what we speak, not in words taught us by human wisdom but in words taught by the Spirit, expressing spiritual truths in spiritual words.* If you want to be a part of Kingdom work that involves offering compassion with redemptive power, then you must be filled with the Spirit of God, there is no other way.

Redemptive Compassion:

I have been under God's teaching, trying to understand and live out redemptive compassion for over twenty years and still find it difficult to explain. There are several additional studies listed on the redemptivecompassion.org website that I hope you investigate as you further seek to understand how God has called us to offer biblical, wholistic help. The following table is a very brief snapshot of some of the differences between what I call Charity Compassion and Redemptive Compassion. I hope it helps bring clarity and understanding to some of these differences.

Charity Compassion	Redemptive Compassion
Sees the need	Sees the person in need
Must relieve pain and suffering	Willing to help carry pain and suffering
Reacts quickly	Responds thoughtfully
Gives what someone wants/asks for	Discerns and gives what one needs
Gives out of their abundance	Gives Christ, the source of abundance
Focuses on immediate relief	Looks for long-term solutions
Offers temporary help	Offers life-transforming help
Gives hand-outs	Gives a hand-up
Sees themselves as the source of help	Sees potential in those with the need
Engages themselves	Partners with and engages the one in need
Believes they have the answer	Knows Christ is the answer
Avoids confrontation	Speaks God's truth, regardless of conflict
Believes they must save people	Believes they must serve people

Questions to Ponder:

1. How does providing resources for people without building resources in people affect those you help?

2. Everyone is leading someone. Who is following you and how are you doing as a godly leader?

3. What challenges might arise from forming partnerships with secular organizations?

4. List some of the differences between charity and redemptive compassion.

⁕ Conclusion

There you have it! Ten premises given to me in a six-week recovery period that initially seemed liked jumbled, disjointed thoughts. It was near the end of week six when I felt the Lord nudge me to say He had given me something to write. But it was two and one-half years later before He nudged again to say, "now it is time to write." The timing felt off as we were in the middle of the COVID-19 pandemic and trying to build a 60 unit housing complex for people in our long-term programs, but the feeling persisted and you're reading the result of my labor.

Assistance has been focused on need, not relationships.

Some have said the philosophy found in Redemptive Compassion is a prophetic word and that might make me some sort of prophet, a term I shy away from. Biblically, prophets tended to bring a warning to people, carrying an unpopular message, that usually made the hearer dislike the carrier as well as the message. Some prophetic messages convicted people to turn from their ways and God relented from sending punishment. Other times, people persisted in their ways and God dealt with them severely. I know these ten premises are hard to digest and I have tried to make them palatable without watering down the truth God has revealed to me. I also know my message and suggested methods are not popular.

I don't claim to be a prophet and I don't know if Redemptive Compassion is a prophetic word for these times, but I do know that for the most part the Church seems to have fallen asleep when it comes to offering compassion that has redemptive power. Confused and unsure how to help people, they have followed the world's methods and played into the enemy's plan. Assistance has been focused on need, not relationships, and the result is an ever increasing population of people reliant on others to provide their daily sustenance, which weakens them and puts them under the control of those who have what they need.

We have not loved as God loves but have loved as the world has said we must. When our love conforms to this world and truth is relative, we have not loved as God loves. When we do not embrace diversity as part of God's creation, we have not loved as God loves. When we tempt with promises of happiness, we have not loved as God loves. When we try to improve lives at the expense of personal improvement, we have not loved as God loves. When we masquerade as the one who can save, in place of the true Savior, we have not loved as God loves. When our help interrupts the plan God has in place, we have not loved as God loves. When our love is random instead of radically planned with God, we have not loved as God loves. When our love stands in place of, or in front of God, we have not loved as God loves. When we take pride in what we can do at the exclusion of what others should do, we have not loved as God loves. When we base our responses on entitlement, we have not loved as God loves.

From my perspective we are confused about how to love others because we do not understand God's love. God's love is restoring not restraining, refining not confining. God's love builds up, often by tearing down, but never permanently keeps one down. God's love purifies and does not pollute our mind, soul and body. God's love has eternity in mind, not present-day comfort and can endure short-term pain for long-term gain. God's love is complete and holy, not competing and full of holes.

The Church must wake up and take notice because the only hope we have is found in the redemptive, restorative love of Jesus Christ. I do not believe there is any other institution, other than the Church, this side of heaven that can understand and offer compassion that has redemptive power. This book was written, not to condemn efforts to date, but to convict, through the power of the Holy Spirit, moving forward. God holds us accountable for what we know and now you know more. Don't take my word on any of this – go to the author of truth and the true source of love – God, to discern your next steps.

I am passionate about educating others on how to help differently – effectively. I have other resources on the topic of Redemptive Compassion and would encourage you to go to redemptivecompassion.org to learn more.

Exodus 3:7-8, paraphrased, has a modern-day message for us, *The Lord said, "I have indeed seen the misery of my people. I have heard them crying out because of their oppressive state of mind and I am concerned about their suffering. So I have come to rescue them from their oppression and bring them out of their poverty mindset and into a good and abundant state of mind, a mindset of wholeness and fullness of life found in me."*

I believe God has a call on the Church to restore and redeem people in His name. Perhaps Exodus 9:16 has been written for us as well as Moses, *"'But I have raised you up for this very purpose, that I might show you my power and that my name might be proclaimed in all the earth.'"*

Let me end with words from our Lord found in Isaiah 49:8-11, *This is what the Lord says: "In the time of my favor I will answer you, and in the day of salvation I will help you; I will keep you and will make you to be a covenant for the people, to restore the land and to reassign its desolate inheritances, to say to the captives, 'Come out,' and to those in darkness, 'Be free!' They will feed beside the roads and find pasture on every barren hill. They will neither hunger nor thirst, nor will the desert heat or the sun beat upon them. He who has compassion on them will guide them and lead them beside springs of water. I will turn all my mountains into roads, and my highways will be raised up."*

About the Author

Lois Tupyi is the Executive Director of Love INC of Treasure Valley. She has worked with the Canyon County based affiliate since April 1999 and assumed the responsibility of Executive Director in January 2002.

Since 2005, Lois has been a trainer for the National Love INC movement. In this capacity she has coordinated and led large group trainings locally and nationally to meet the training needs of developing affiliates.

Love INC of Treasure Valley's campus is a training site for people in all stages of their Love INC ministry growth as well as others interested in learning more about Redemptive Compassion. Lois is an inspiring speaker and educator at area churches and communities across the nation, frequently traveling to share her passion for the biblical call to wholistic help.

Lois is the author of the Redemptive Compassion Study Guide, an eight-week study on the biblical call to wholistic help. Along with the study book are class DVDs, student hand-outs and a leader's guide to help facility conversation on how to help differently - redemptively. Lois has also written Affirming Potential, a twelve-week class designed to help participants examine their life and apply concepts found in the Dream Tool, which helps them set and achieve dreams and goals to reach their God-given potential.

Lois is the author of the bestseller, *Selah: Pause and Consider*. Her unique devotional encourages personal worship and spiritual growth through daily Bible reading, praise music, and beautiful photography.

An Idaho native, Lois and her husband reside on a small Hereford ranch in Wilder, where they enjoy the rural lifestyle. She has three adult children and fourteen beautiful grandchildren.

Go to the website *redemptivecompassion.org* to learn more about all of the Redemptive Compassion components, including video excerpts from the training DVDs. Email *redemptivecompassion@gmail.com* for information on how to bring Lois to your community or additional classroom training opportunities with her.